Miracles in the Marketplace

McDougal & Associates
Servants of Christ and Stewards of the
Mysteries of God

Miracles in the Marketplace

Tales of an Unlikely Lawyer

BY

ALEXANDER WATSON, ESQ.

Miracles in the Marketplace: Tales of an Unlikely Lawyer
Copyright © 2025 — Alexander Watson
ALL RIGHTS RESERVED

Unless otherwise noted, all Scripture quotations are from the *Holy Bible, New King James Version* © copyright 1979, 1980, 1982 by Thomas Nelson, Inc., Nashville, Tennessee. References marked NIV are from *The Holy Bible, New International Version*, copyright © 1973, 1978, 1984, 2011 by Biblica, Colorado Springs, Colorado. References marked NLT are from *The New Living Translation of the Bible,* copyright © 1996 by Tyndale House Publishers, Inc., Wheaton, Illinois. All rights reserved. Used by permission.

Published by:

McDougal & Associates
www.thepublishedword.com

McDougal & Associates is dedicated to spreading the Gospel of the Lord Jesus Christ to as many people as possible in the shortest time possible.

ISBN 978-1-964665-13-9 Trade Paper Version
ISBN 978-1-96465-15-3 Hardback Version

Printed on demand in the U.S., the U.K. and Australia
For Worldwide Distribution

Dedication

To my lovely wife, Emily, my life partner and best friend.

"Call to Me, and I will answer you, and show you great and mighty things, which you do not know."

– God in Jeremiah 33:3

Contents

Author's Foreword 9

Part 1: Miracles in the Marketplace 11
   Head in the Clouds, Feet on the Ground 13
   Law School 16
   My Appearance Before Judge Mahon 20
   The Reluctant Evangelist 23
   The Answer to Everything 26
   The Holy Spirit, Our Secret Agent 33
   The Holy Spirit, the Helper 40
   What Do You Have from Heaven? 43
   Base Camp 45
   A Municipal Court Appearance 49
   Miracles in the Marketplace 52
   Let the Holy Spirit Do His Work 56
   Where's the Fruit? 65
   "Words Will Be As Cheap As Water" 71
   Your Work Shall Be Rewarded 73
   Can a Christian Be a Lawyer? 79
   Jesus Dealt with the Sin Problem 85
   Continuous Blessing 88
   Elijah's Restoration 95
   You Will See Greater Things 99
   The Challenge of Isaiah 61 104

Foolishness vs Wisdom 110
　　An Extraordinary Life 114
　　Single or Married? 117
　　An Amazing Birthday Present 120

Part 2: Visions and Prophecies from the Holy Spirit 123
　　Introduction 124
　　A Ribbon from Heaven 125
　　Different Mountaintops 127
　　An Offering Converted to a Blessing 129
　　The Tablets of Your Heart 131
　　Jeremiah, Ezekiel, Daniel and Jesus 133
　　Snow in the Spring 136
　　The Bottom of the Cross 137
　　Distributing Mantles 139
　　A Man Healed 141
　　The Marriage Ceremony 142
　　Trust the Lighthouse 144
　　The Receiver 145
　　Faces Like Lions 148
　　Standing at the Red Sea 149
　　A Trail To the Villages 150
　　Waves 151
　　Army of God 153
　　Scrolls in Heaven 158
　　The Skull 160

Part 3: An Invitation 163
　　My Invitation 165

　　Author Contact Page 167

Author's Foreword

Through the years, it has been my privilege to represent many fascinating clients: Princeton professors, Grammy and Emmy winners, Einstein's colleagues and students, conductors at Carnegie Hall, rock stars, pilots, Tictoc stars, wealthy owners of internet companies, FBI and CIA agents, federal marshals, and even a gubernatorial candidate. However, to me, the most impressive of all was a part-time usher at the Lincoln Center in New York. She had the privilege of standing on stage behind the side curtain, getting performers ready to make an entrance, and she told remarkable stories of the Rolling Stones, Tony Bennett, the Beatles, Johnny Cash, Linda Ronstadt, the Beach Boys, Pavarotti, and countless others. Some were gracious, like Diana Ross, and some were prima donnas. When the curtain went up, it was her responsibility to bring the performer on stage and watch from the wings.

I felt a certain kinship with that woman. I have sometimes been called "The Miracle Man" for my work with clients, but it is Jesus who is the real Miracle Worker. It is now my job to be like that usher and introduce you to the real Miracle-Worker, Jesus Christ, and bring Him from offstage. I hope that through these simple stories, you, the reader, will meet Him for who He really is. There are many tales to tell, and I must get to it.

My writings are divided into two parts. Part 1 consists of stories and meditations about Jesus' work in my life. Part 2 consists of visions I was blessed to see and prophecies I was blessed to deliver at various times and places. May they be a blessing to you too.

Alexander Watson
Attorney at Law

PART 1

MIRACLES IN THE MARKETPLACE

HEAD IN THE CLOUDS, FEET ON THE GROUND

Years ago, I heard someone say, "God wants people with their head in the clouds and their feet on the ground." In other words, He wants His people to grow to their full spiritual height. He wants people who know His voice (having their head in the clouds), but who are also firmly rooted to practical life (having their feet on the ground). In my youth I desperately wanted to be a pastor, but my pastor asked me, "What life experience do you have to impart to others? What authority would you have with them?" He was right. I needed some life experience. I needed to have my feet firmly planted on the ground.

Since I was apparently not called to preach, I needed a secular job, but my advisor at Princeton sneered at me, laughed, and gave me no advice. It was a humiliating experience.

I thought I might become a missionary to Africa, but I seemed to have no skills to offer there either. I applied at a missionary school in England, but they wisely refused me admission. My own father, whose job it was to hire engineers at Pratt and Whitney, told me he wouldn't hire me. I was, in his words, "Good fer nothin.'" (I can count on one hand the times he spent with me.)

I worked my way through law school, sometimes keeping up with three part-time jobs and going to school full-time. That experience alone would fill a book. God never seemed to come through for me. Things were just "all right." There were no major breakthroughs or unusual provisions.

Then one night I was the first person to arrive at the scene of a four-car head-on collision. After taking care of victims who were walking around dazed, I could hear a faint whimper from a distance: "Help us! Somebody help us!" As I looked for the source of the sound, I saw that the fourth car had driven off the side of the road into the woods, and the engine was on fire. The car was lying on its side on the passenger door, and, apparently, the passengers were still inside. Again I heard from the car: "Please help us!"

At this point, all the frustrations came to the surface, the frustrations of unanswered prayers and no results, no power, no breakthroughs, and no miracles. I shouted "JESUS, YOU HAVE GOT TO DO SOMETHING—RIGHT NOW!" At that moment, everything changed. Jesus *is* real! Miracles started to happen for me.

The hood of the vehicle had been torn off in the accident. That was fortunate, because the fire was exposed, and I could walk right up to the engine. I hoped to smother the fire with my jacket. Instead, the jacket went up in flames. Other people began to arrive, but no one wanted to get close to the burning car. None had a fire extinguisher, but someone had a bucket of water.

It is common knowledge that you're not supposed to use water on a gasoline fire, but something in me told me to try it. I figured that if I had enough water and got close enough to the source of the flames, I could starve the fire of oxygen long enough to put it out. It worked for a few minutes, and another guy and I quickly began to look to see if we could take care of the people inside the car.

The roof of the car had been torn off in the accident, and the vehicle was an instant convertible. The four passengers were still strapped in and dangling on their side, held in place by their shoulder harnesses.

The fire reignited, but we were able to carefully carry the conscious passengers out one by one. An ambulance arrived, and the medics were able to take care of the one unconscious passenger still in the car. The next day the newspaper reported that there had been no fatalities from that horrendous accident. Praise God! He came through for me when there seemed to be no way, and He has been doing miracles for me ever since.

Law School

In the spring semester of my third and final year of law school, the last semester before entering the work force, I took my Evidence class. The professor, whose name I have long since forgotten, literally wrote the book on Evidence, and he loved the subtle nuances of the law.

At the time, as I noted in the previous chapter, I was working three part-time jobs to support myself, and in addition to Evidence, I had three or four other equally demanding courses. Every night we were tasked with reading four or five cases for each of these classes. The opinions were not long, usually four to five pages each, but they were terse and complex. The judge's opinions rested on his or her interpretation of the facts and the law. Change the facts slightly, and the holding would be turned on its head. Change the laws or the jurisdiction, and the holding would turn again.

One day the professor called on me to answer his questions on the case at hand. Not having spoken to anyone about the case, I simply could not answer him. Tongue-tied and sleep deprived, I could not seem to process the answer.

You have to understand that I was not brought up by lawyers who enjoyed debating the issues of the day at the dinner table. I was always told to be quiet and listen. In any event, I was not able to engage the professor in a debate.

As my tired brain tried to formulate a response, the professor said, "Well, Mr. Watson, it seems you have not read the case or if you have, you are frozen in fear. Let's change the facts."

He then proceeded to change the fact pattern and asked, "How would these new facts impact the judge's holding?" Hands went up all over the room, but the professor kept looking at me. When I still could not answer, I thought he would eventually move on to someone else. He didn't. He criticized me, and then questioned further: "What would the holding be under these new sets of facts?" Again the question went unanswered.

"Mr. Watson," he asked, "did you read the next case?

"Yes," I replied

"Then what is the holding of the next case, and what was the judge's rationale?" he asked.

I turned the page and saw that I had indeed read the case, but just as I began to formulate an answer, he asked: "Mr. Watson, what if we change the facts in such and such a way. How would the judge rule in that case? What if the case was brought in federal court, and the Federal Rules of

Evidence applied. How would the holding differ?" Again, hands went up all around the room.

"All right, Mr. Watson, let's go on to the next case." This went on for the full fifty-minute class, from the first minute to the last. Then, he picked up with me again the next day and the next, for five whole days. Law students tend to be competitive, so none of the other students offered me any assistance. The rest of my grades were fine, but, as a result of that class, the academic committee forced me to take a year off and return for another semester based solely upon my poor verbal performance.

Interestingly enough, when I returned to the law school at the beginning of the next year, I visited the Registrar's office and found the halls filled with third-year law students. They were lined up to withdraw from that particular professor's Evidence class. It seems that they had heard the rumors about his cruel treatment of a certain student during the previous semester. Since no one was willing to take his class, the great professor was forced to take a year's leave of absence himself.

I was apparently unsuited for law school and the law, but God used that experience to mold me. And although I failed miserably and was humiliated in work and in my personal life, through it all I lost my fear of failure and gained a new-found confidence that God was with me. Even in the most difficult times and the lonely times to follow, I knew His presence.

When you go through such experiences, you learn that God will never leave you, and even failure is not the end. It's just a stepping stone to greater things. As the apostle Paul wrote to the Corinthian believers:

> *For you see your calling, brethren, that not many wise according to the flesh, not many mighty, not many noble, are called. But God has chosen the foolish things of the world to put to shame the wise, and God has chosen the weak things of the world to put to shame the things which are mighty; and the base things of the world and the things which are despised God has chosen, and the things which are not, to bring to nothing the things that are, that no flesh should glory in His presence. But of Him you are in Christ Jesus, who became for us wisdom from God – and righteousness and sanctification and redemption – that, as it is written, "He who glories, let him glory in the Lord."* 1 Corinthians 1:26-31

I can say AMEN to that.

My Appearance Before Judge Mahon

There are many biblical principles which apply to the practice of law. The book of Proverbs, for example, shows us not only how to grow to maturity, but also how to govern and how to conduct a successful business:

When a man's ways please the Lord,
He makes even his enemies to be at peace with him.
Proverbs 16:7

The words of Jesus are full of wisdom for our daily lives:

Therefore, whatever you want men to do to you, do also to them, for this is the Law and the Prophets.
Matthew 7:12

The letters to the churches of the New Testament, likewise, give us many helpful teachings:

My Appearance Before Judge Mahon

If your enemy is hungry, feed him;
If he is thirsty, give him a drink;
For in so doing you will heap coals of fire on his head.
Romans 12:20

On one motion day, I had to appear before Judge Mahon in Somerset County Superior Court on a motion to compel my adversary to produce certain documents in a litigation matter. The opposing attorney, whose name I have forgotten, was the caricature of a nasty litigator, impossible to deal with in any normal fashion and completely rude. That was why I had to bring the matter before Judge Mahon in the first place.

As we began to state our respective positions, Judge Mahon quickly saw that it would be contentious and asked us to meet him in chambers. I could see that the judge had dealt with my adversary on numerous occasions and that there was no love lost between them.

Once in chambers, since I represented the plaintiff, Judge Mahon asked me first what I was looking for. Normally, this is the time when attorneys fight like cats and dogs outside the hearing of the general public, and the judge has to listen to a barrage of bitter complaints from both sides and rule like a parent over fighting children. As soon as I recognized that the judge hated my adversary already, the Holy Spirit gave me a new approach and I totally changed my tactics.

"Your Honor," I said, "my adversary has been a very good person to work with so far. He has agreed to almost everything I asked. He has been a great gentlemen and an honor to our profession throughout these proceedings, but all I need is for him to produce a few documents."

As I said that, the judge actually did a triple-take. He looked at me, and then the other guy three times because he couldn't believe what was coming out of my mouth. He didn't know me, but he knew what kind of person the other attorney was. He didn't bother to listen to the opposing argument, and what he said next really surprised me. "Mr. Watson, I'll give you whatever you want."

God is absolutely awesome! He knows how to get every job done.

THE RELUCTANT EVANGELIST

During the Gulf War, I met with a refugee from Iraq to discuss her estate planning. Instead of a forty-five minute consultation, we talked for two and half hours. She told me about the children's books she had written concerning the Judeo-Christian history of her country. She described Iraq as "the Other Holy Land." Jonah the prophet had preached in Ninevah (near where Bagdad is today), not just once, but several times, and a Christian church was established there as early as 300 A.D. In fact, in years past, Jonah had been held in high regard by Iraqis. A tooth from the great fish was displayed in a museum in Bagdad, and Jonah was buried nearby. No doubt that's all gone today.

Jonah had the common Jewish worldview held at that time that God was only concerned about the Israelites. Israel will always be the "apple of God's eye," and He will never abandon His people. But God had to break Jonah out of his limited view. He told Jonah:

> *"Arise, go to Nineveh, that great city, and cry out against it; for their wickedness has come up before Me."*   Jonah 1:2

Naturally, Jonah rebelled at God's call for him to preach repentance to Ninevah. If you walked into the city in Jonah's day, you would see the heads of Iraqi enemies impaled on stakes along the path. Jonah fled this calling and boarded a ship to Tarshish.

Then, while he was on the boat, a storm arose, and he confessed to the crew that he was running away from God's call. The shipmates had heard of this powerful God, and they asked His forgiveness as they threw Jonah overboard.

The idea that God cared about Gentiles was abhorrent to Jonah. Wasn't He "the God of Abraham, Isaac, and Jacob?" The idea that God wanted the Assyrians to repent was unthinkable. In the same way, I believe parts of His Church need to break out of their mistaken impression that God is only concerned with those inside the Church. They attend church services, regional conferences, and hear more and more teaching, but they never leave the comfort of their pews. Jonah finally came to his senses:

> *"When my soul fainted within me,*
> *I remembered the Lord;*
> *And my prayer went up to You,*
> *Into Your holy temple.*
> *Those who regard worthless idols*
> *Forsake their own Mercy.*
> *But I will sacrifice to You*

> *With the voice of thanksgiving;*
> *I will pay what I have vowed.*
> *Salvation is of the Lord."*
> *So the Lord spoke to the fish, and it vomited Jonah onto dry land.* Jonah 2:7-10

Jonah simply preached the "word" God gave him. It wasn't a complicated "evangelical sermon" we would think about today. He was to preach: "Yet forty days, and Nineveh shall be overthrown!" (Jonah 3:4). It is preaching the words God gives us rather than our own thoughts that brings repentance. The apostle Paul wrote:

> *But if all prophesy, and an unbeliever or an uninformed person comes in, he is convinced by all, he is convicted by all. And thus the secrets of his heart are revealed; and so, falling down on his face, he will worship God and report that God is truly among you.* 1 Corinthians 14: 24-25

Jonah had such a powerful, simple message. When God's Word is released, it *"breaks the rock"* (Jeremiah 23:29). It brings people to repentance and changes the atmosphere.

THE ANSWER TO EVERYTHING

And He [Jesus] said to them, "Which of you shall have a friend, and go to him at midnight and say to him, 'Friend, lend me three loaves; for a friend of mine has come to me on his journey, and I have nothing to set before him'; and he will answer from within and say, 'Do not trouble me; the door is now shut, and my children are with me in bed; I cannot rise and give to you'? I say to you, though he will not rise and give to him because he is his friend, yet because of his persistence he will rise and give him as many as he needs.

"So I say to you, ask, and it will be given to you; seek, and you will find; knock, and it will be opened to you. For everyone who asks receives, and he who seeks finds, and to him who knocks it will be opened. If a son asks for bread from any father among you, will he give him a stone? Or if he asks for a fish, will he give him a serpent instead of a fish? Or if he asks for an egg, will he offer him a scorpion? If you then, being evil, know how to give good gifts to your children, how much more will your heavenly Father give the Holy Spirit to those who ask Him!" Luke 11:5-13

I have often spent time with the Lord in my personal devotions late at night. One such night, at about midnight, I heard the Lord say, "I will give you the answer to everything."

My first thought was that either this was the enemy talking or these words were coming from my own head. I said, "Lord, if this is You, tell me again in the morning," and I went to bed.

Amazingly, the first thing in the morning, during my time with the Lord, He showed me Luke 11:5-13 and that was it.

In this passage, Jesus spoke about a friend. There are different kinds of friends. Some people we call "friends" are just acquaintances, and you know you could never ask them for anything. Others are indeed friends in the best sense, and you know you can ask them for help. Once I asked a young assistant pastor to help me move some boxes, as part of my move to a new house near his church. He looked down at me as if to say, "How dare you ask me for help with that menial task!"

That was okay. I knew I had other friends who would show up, and we would have a good time together moving my things. I had faith in those friends because of the nature of our relationship.

When someone asks us for help, our first response is often, "I don't have any (no bread, for instance)." When I worked as a student assistant pastor at the Grenfell

Mission in Maine for two summers, I had a number of teenagers who came to me for advice. I was only about twenty myself, practically still a teenager, and yet one girl came to me asking me to give her a reason she should not commit suicide. Certain horrible things had happened to her, and she no longer wanted to live. I told her I needed to think about that and I'd give her the answer the next day.

The next day, I still wasn't sure what I should tell her, but she came up to me eager to hear my answer. A thought came to me, and I said, "You came back today because you hoped I would give you the answer. What I can say is that tomorrow is your answer. Tomorrow is your reason to live. Tomorrow is a new day and with it comes new possibilities. As long as you have a tomorrow, you will have new possibilities." She was quite happy with that answer.

The thing is: GOD WILL ANSWER! According to the Scriptures, the man said, *"Do not trouble me. The door is now shut."* If you are like I was, you may feel like the door is *always* shut, and God is not willing help you. You may be thinking, "I come from the wrong side of the tracks. God is not coming through because of me. He would open the door for someone else, but not for *me*. I'm not a pastor, I'm not an apostle, prophet, or teacher. I don't have the gift of healing. If I was good enough, He would have called me to those roles."

But the thing is He WILL ANSWER, and He will answer YOU! He will answer, because you are His child and also because of your persistence, your excessive boldness. The man finally said, "Take it all, I'm going back to bed."

Jesus concluded, *"If you then, being evil, know how to give good gifts to your children, how much more will your heavenly Father ...."* I'm so glad He knows me, so evil, so "messed up." His answer, however, is not based on our righteousness, but on His goodness.

It is as Jesus said to Nicodemus, *"You must be born again"* (John 3:7). Every one of us who has tried so hard to follow the Law, to be good, comes to the point where he or she says, "I can't do it. I can't get this right. I can't live my life right. Lord, in order for me to walk with You, You will have to help me start all over again. Take me back to the womb, for I need to be born again."

"How much more will your heavenly Father give the Holy Spirit to those who ask Him." This thought seems to be out of place, but Luke was saying that the Holy Spirit is the ultimate and complete answer to what you are asking for. It's in the Person that the answer is found. *He* is the key to everything, especially everything you need in the Kingdom of God.

When the Panama Canal was finally opened in 1914, the whole Pacific was opened to the Western world. Through this one gateway, the East and West were connected. In the same way, there is a single Person who is the answer. With the Holy Spirit, we can be given our marching orders. We can be led. We can enjoy the Kingdom of God and live in all its aspects—financial provision, healing, wholesome and rewarding relationships, an abundant life.

The Holy Spirit is the answer to living in the Kingdom. He brings us into holiness and repentance, changing us from the inside out. He is not our servant, but we are His. It is the Father's good pleasure to give us the Kingdom (see Luke 12:32) and to transform us to live in that Kingdom.

When the Comforter comes into our lives, He will do all of the following:

1. He tells us God's thoughts (see 1 Corinthians 2:11 and Amos 4:13).
2. He gives us the understanding of God's free gifts (see 1 Corinthians 2:12).
3. He gives us the words to express spiritual truths (see 1 Corinthians 2:15).
4. He enables us to accept the things that come from God (see 1 Corinthians 2:14).
5. He gives us understanding of these things from God (see 1 Corinthians 2:14).
6. He takes us through the painful process of growing up into holiness. This incudes chastising us (see Hebrews 12:6).
7. He gives us the ability to judge all things (see 1 Corinthians 2:15).
8. He makes us not subject to other's judgments (see 1 Corinthians 2:15).

9. He gives us the mind of Christ (see 1 Corinthians 2:16).
10. He takes what belongs to Jesus and gives it to us (see John 17).
11. He teaches us all things (see 1 John 2:27).
12. He redeems us so that the blessing of Abraham might come to the Gentiles through Christ Jesus (see Galatians 3:14).

By faith, we can receive the promise of the Spirit. Jesus didn't just give us a list of answers to our problems; He gave us a Person to abide with us, to teach, convict, and transform us.

When I worked as a student assistant pastor in Maine, I found myself involved with a very liberal church organization. It had started as an evangelical mission to the sailors and fisherman in Northern Maine and Nova Scotia, but had long since lost its evangelical roots and fervor. As a university student during the summers of 1973 and 74, I was given the opportunity to preach at up to four small churches every Sunday when the pastor was on vacation. As I noted earlier, I had long wanted to be a preacher, so I accepted this opportunity enthusiastically, and it didn't matter to me what denomination the people were.

When my time came, I spoke about the two most important things in my life — the cross of Jesus Christ and the work and Person of the Holy Spirit in our lives. I enthusiastically spoke about the Holy Spirit as a Person we could know. The young people responded, but not everyone was happy with my messages.

One Sunday, during the greeting time after the service, the senior deacon cornered me. He said, "There are only three churches in this town: the Baptists, the Pentecostals, and us. If people want to get saved, they go to the Baptist church. If they want to speak in tongues, they go to the Assemblies of God. We cater to everyone else.[1] The last person who preached here like you do, we made him stop preaching and voted him out DURING the message."

Not surprisingly, this deacon never came back to my services again, so he missed hearing more about Jesus, the cross, and Jesus' best friend, the Holy Spirit, who is the answer to everything.

---

1. Yes, he said, "we cater."

The Holy Spirit, Our Secret Agent

Now the king of Syria was making war against Israel; and he consulted with his servants, saying, "My camp will be in such and such a place." And the man of God sent to the king of Israel, saying, "Beware that you do not pass this place, for the Syrians are coming down there." Then the king of Israel sent someone to the place of which the man of God had told him. Thus he warned him, and he was watchful there, not just once or twice.
Therefore the heart of the king of Syria was greatly troubled by this thing; and he called his servants and said to them, "Will you not show me which of us is for the king of Israel?"   2 Kings 6:8-10

God revealed to Elisha when and where the Syrians were preparing to attack, and He did this *"not just once or twice."* You and I are also in a war, and the Holy Spirit is our Secret Agent. He doesn't just point us to Himself; He actually gives us an unfair advantage over our enemies in every situation.

MIRACLES IN THE MARKETPLACE

The King of Syria sent an entire army to capture Elisha, and they surrounded the city where he was staying. Elisha's servant went outside early that morning, and when he saw this Syrian army, he went running back to Elisha in a panic. Sometimes our enemies seem overwhelming.

> *And it was told him [the king of Syria], saying, "Surely he is in Dothan."*
> *Therefore he sent horses and chariots and a great army there, and they came by night and surrounded the city. And when the servant of the man of God arose early and went out, there was an army, surrounding the city with horses and chariots. And his servant said to him, "Alas, my master! What shall we do?"* 2 Kings 6:13-15

Elisha prayed for the servant that he would have the ability to see the unseen forces arrayed on their behalf, to see the spiritual dimension which had been there for them all the time. And it worked:

> *So he [Elisha] answered, "Do not fear, for those who are with us are more than those who are with them." And Elisha prayed, and said, "LORD, I pray, open his eyes that he may see." Then the LORD opened the eyes of the young man, and he saw. And behold, the mountain was full of horses and chariots of fire all around Elisha.*
> 2 Kings 6:16-17

The solution God provides is always new and outside the box. He is not locked into any set formula. He will do His work in different ways.

Elijah had called fire down on soldiers, but Elisha prayed, instead, that his enemies be blinded. Then he led them by the hand to Samaria.

> *So when the Syrians came down to him, Elisha prayed to the* Lord, *and said, "Strike this people, I pray, with blindness." And He struck them with blindness according to the word of Elisha.*
> *Now Elisha said to them, "This is not the way, nor is this the city. Follow me, and I will bring you to the man whom you seek." But he led them to Samaria.*
>
> 2 Kings 6:18-9

When we cry out to God, He provides. Sometimes it is in secret, but, again, it is always outside the box.

We need this revelation that God's ways are outside the box. His resources are available to us to prevail against any and every enemy. We need to see into this Kingdom realm.

When Peter and Jesus owed taxes, Jesus provided the coin in the fish's mouth for Peter to catch (see Matthew 17:24-27). Such hidden resources of Kingdom living make others scratch their heads. It was normal for Elisha, and it should be normal for us today as well.

If you don't see a solution, cry out to God to open your eyes or to open the eyes of another who is not yet seeing the Kingdom as a resource.

A certain client of mine, a surveyor, called me to say he had made a serious error on a commercial survey he had prepared for a long-time client, a builder. The builder wanted thousands of dollars in damages and was prepared to sue to get it.

I received a call from the opposing attorney, and it became clear that he was approaching this case like an attack dog—threatening my client with triple damages and attorney's fees. He said, "These two parties have worked together for more than twenty years as friends, but your client not only made a terrible mistake; he refused to offer to pay the damages. He just went on his merry way as if nothing had happened. We attorneys are going to make a lot of money on this case."

I couldn't see the man, of course, but I could almost imagine him drooling with excitement. What should I do now?

I got an idea and called my client. I told him it seemed to me that what the other side wanted, more than anything else, was an apology. He said he would gladly apologize ... if I thought that would work.

The other attorney was waiting on our proposal for settlement, so I called him back. I said, "My client will apologize in open court and will continue working with the plaintiff. That is our offer."

There was dead silence on the other end of the line, and I wondered if the opposing attorney had maybe hit the floor. When he finally spoke, he asked, "But how much money are you offering?"

"No money," I said. "These men are long-time friends. He will just apologize."

In every settlement negotiation, the opposing attorney is compelled to take any offer to his client, no matter how ridiculous it might seem. Amazingly, I got a call back within a few minutes accepting this offer. Thank You, God!

Sometimes the answer we need comes from a surprising place. Once I was Counsel to the Board of an assisted living facility in Pennsylvania. The executive director was a wonderful energetic lady who had great rapport with all the residents. She was well versed in medical issues, but she fell short when it came to legal or financial matters. A "recall notice" had come about their sprinkler system. It was seriously defective and created an extremely dangerous situation. The company that supplied the sprinkler units was willing to provide a complete replacement for all two hundred and fifty of them at no cost. Unfortunately, the recall period had lapsed. Now the replacement cost, about $450,000, would have to be borne by the facility. This was money they did not have, so the Board turned to me for answers.

I really didn't have an answer, so I said, "Let's table this question for a month and see what we can come up with in the meantime." This gave me time to pray and ask God for His help!

Any disclosure of this matter to the residents would be catastrophic for business, but in this case, it was necessary. We had no choice. We were in a serious bind, but I knew that God would do something extraordinary as we trusted Him.

When the Board arrived for the next meeting, they all solemnly turned to me for some words of wisdom. If we couldn't find some solution, the home might have to declare bankruptcy. I wasn't sure how, but I had a sense that God was about to perform a miracle for us. Wisdom settled over me, and I sensed that Jesus was there, seated at the table with us.

We were all in for a major surprise. It quickly turned out that someone we knew had dealings with the sprinkler company, and through this professional connection and through some wrangling, the company agreed to replace all the sprinklers without charge—even though the warranty had expired.

Sometimes God surprises us with an unexpected miracle, and this brings unexpected joys and wonderful solutions that we could not have arranged ourselves. This is why *He* gets all the credit. We surely can't figure everything out for ourselves.

You may have many examples of how God has come through for you. Keep expecting. Keep asking. Keep crying out to Him when you need answers. He will never fail you.

When an angel visited Daniel, he said, *"Don't be afraid, Daniel. Since the first day you began to pray for understanding and to humble yourself before your God, your request has been heard in heaven. I have come in answer to your prayer"* (Daniel 10:12, NLT). What are we expressing to God? Are we asking Him for more? Are we asking Him for miracles? Are we calling out to Him?

The Comforter (the Holy Spirit) has been sent to comfort us, but we don't need His comfort when we're resting in our easy chair sipping lemonade. When we need Him is when we're out doing new things for Him in many different capacities and we're confronted by enemies or difficult situations. He is always there for us! Yes, He never fails!

The Holy Spirit, the Helper

The New King James Bible translates John 15:26 as follows:

> But when the Helper comes, whom I shall send to you from the Father, the Spirit of truth, who proceeds from the Father, He will testify of Me.

One summer when I was young, I worked as a laborer for a mason in our town. I carried 6" and 12" concrete blocks to the construction site, cleaned the shovels and cement mixer at the end of the day, and cleaned the blocks after they had been laid. Toward the end of the summer, I was trusted to run the mixer to prepare the mortar, but always under supervision. I never actually laid blocks, which takes years of experience. I was just a "helper," a "grunt," a "laborer."

If we think of the Holy Spirit in this same way, as just as our "Helper," we misunderstand the full measure of His role. Of course He is our Helper, but He is also God, our Attorney, Counselor, and Advocate (see 1 John 2:1).

He provides effective prayers when we don't know how to pray (see Romans 8:26), and He does many other wonderful things for us. The word used to describe Him in the Bible, *parakletos*, can be translated as "Helper," but it can also be translated as "One called to one's side" or "Counselor" or "Advocate." The commentary in the Bible I use says on this point: "In nonbiblical literature, *parakletos* had the technical meaning of an attorney who appears in court on another's behalf."[1]

Clearly, Jesus said that the Holy Spirit would stand in on His behalf:

And I will pray the Father and He will give you another Helper, that he will abide with you forever. John 14:16

On this point, the commentary in my Bible says another Helper means "one just like Me. He will do in My absence what I would do if I were physically present with you."[2]

In Africa, slaves that were to be moved from place to place were attached to each other with leg irons. Shackled in this way, they had to walk hundreds of miles to the coast, for instance, to be picked up by slave ships taking them to the New World. Often, an exhausted slave would fall to the ground to the right or left, still held by the leg

---

1. *The New Spirit-Filled Life Bible*, Nashville, Tennessee (Thomas Nelson: 2020).
2. Ibid

irons. The man behind would try to help him up, but the only way to do so was to fall over on purpose—still held by leg irons. Only then could he help his exhausted companion up. Since the Bible translators had no word to express the depth of the Holy Spirit's work, they used an African word from the Xhosa language for a person who comes alongside to help another up. This is the work of the Holy Spirit. He comes alongside us to help us up.

WHAT DO YOU HAVE FROM HEAVEN?

And they said to Him, "By what authority are You doing these things? And who gave You this authority to do these things?" But Jesus answered and said to them, "I also will ask you one question; then answer Me, and I will tell you by what authority I do these things: The baptism of John — was it from heaven or from men? Answer Me."

And they reasoned among themselves, saying, "If we say, 'From heaven,' He will say, 'Why then did you not believe him?' But if we say, 'From men' " — they feared the people, for all counted John to have been a prophet indeed. So they answered and said to Jesus, "We do not know."

And Jesus answered and said to them, "Neither will I tell you by what authority I do these things."   Mark 11:28-33

These people asked Jesus, "Who gave You authority to do these things?" and you will have to answer that same question. Real authority comes from God Himself. He is your Secret Agent, working behind the scenes. He gives authority to people you wouldn't expect:

Our victory is not dependent upon our education, our connections, or our history. We will have to get used to resentment from certain quarters because God gives us an unfair advantage. He fights for us.

God wants to put you in a position where you don't fear a boss or an organization, but you look to Him for your place in society, in a job, in a marriage, or in any other situation. Advancement and promotion come from God alone (see Psalm 75:6-7).

Was the authority Jesus displayed from Heaven or from men? Clearly, we need to look to Heaven for the answers we need. God gives us new and creative thoughts for answers to math problems, new computer programs, new engineering solutions, or whatever else is needed. Heaven will give you the ability to solve problems, manage money, and start a ministry or a business.

In my law practice, God gave me new ways to describe tax implications for families. He showed me how to use spreadsheets and diagrams to make taxes easy to understand and gave me simple, streamlined solutions to complicated financial problems. He provided all this, so He gets all the glory.

The ministries of Jesus and John the Baptist were so different, but both came from Heaven. Your vocation in life will look different too. What has Heaven given you? What will Heaven give you in the days ahead? Be expectant and receive the unique solutions God's Spirit offers.

BASE CAMP

As you may know, a base camp is the starting point to a great climb. The base camp on Mount Everest is already at 17,598 feet. Climbers spend a few days there to acclimatize themselves to the thinner air before moving out to higher elevations. The base camp is the place to stock up on food and equipment and make sure your supplies are sufficient for the trip ahead. Being at the base camp allows you to look up at the mountain and dream about the next few days of hiking.

I took a high school group from my church to hike Mount Katahdin in Maine. This mountain is at the very end of the Appalachian Trail and, to many, it is the highlight of the whole trail. It's the tallest peak in Maine and one of the tallest on the East Coast.

This was going to be a five day trip — one day hiking up to the base camp, and four days to the summit and along the ridge route and down the other side of the mountain. The first day was easy, only two to three miles to the base camp. There we had a magnificent view of Katahdin and the ridge route, which loomed above.

Our reservations at the lodge included a hot meal, comfortable bunk beds, and a hearty breakfast. However, after the last bite of that meal, the reality set in for some of my campers. We were going to leave the comfort of that lodge and hike for the next four days and three nights in the wilderness. They could see the mountain looming before them, and the thought of making our way into that wilderness suddenly seemed very daunting.

Not surprisingly, several in our group volunteered to stay at the base camp. The view from there was great, the fireplace was warm and inviting, and they wouldn't have to make a bed on the ground on some distant trail. "And what if it rained?" they were wondering.

I had to disabuse them of this dream. "Unfortunately," I said, "we will not be coming back this way, so there would be no one to pick you up. And it's a very long walk back to Bangor. Besides, we don't have reservations for tomorrow, and the place is booked. Someone else needs your bed." That ended their dream.

Jesus bought for us a wonderful life. He said, *"I have come that they may have life, and that they may have it more abundantly"* (John 10:10). Some translations say, "I will give them an extraordinary life, a superabundant life or *zoë* life." (*Zoë* is the Greek word that describes the uniquely wonderful life that God gives). Jesus took care of the sin problem—redeeming us so we could have this life, forgiven and free, truly free.

But some are comfortable at the base camp—being forgiven, enjoying the view, watching others go forward, but never venturing out into this extraordinary life themselves. When Jesus comes into our lives, He saves us and gives us a taste of new wine, and when He baptizes us with the Holy Spirit, He does it for a reason. The Comforter isn't with us simply to make us comfortable. He is our Comforter when we're out there struggling, suffering, and pushing ahead. He comforts us on our journey and in our work.

Those who wanted to stay at the base camp had the view looking up at the mountain, but if they had stayed behind, they would never have seen the greater views from the top of the mountain, looking over the rest of Maine. The base camp looked very small and insignificant from that much higher ridge.

As we set out on those four days of adventure, we saw many things—bears, deer, other folks on the trail, and other vistas—as we crossed over. The base camp was long forgotten. It had only been a starting point, not our destination.

One prophet who had an extraordinary life was Jonah. God took him on a wild ride—literally. After three days of misery, he had a great story to tell. When Jonah finally came to his senses and agreed to do what he was called to do, he said: *"Those who follow worthless idols forfeit the grace of God that could be theirs"* (Jonah 2:8, My Paraphrase). This means those who choose to stay at the base camp never experience the greater joys and the depths of the real life God offers.

If you have accepted Jesus as your Savior, you can rely on many things—His forgiveness, His faithfulness to you wherever you go, His friendship in whatever you do, and His provision for whatever work your hands employ. Understanding that truth is your "base camp." Now what are you going to do with it? What trail will you choose?

A MUNICIPAL COURT APPEARANCE

All attorneys are required to do some *pro bono* work. On one occasion I was assigned a case by the Bar Association in which my client had been charged with a serious motor vehicle offense. He came to my office to talk about it. The first thing he said was that he was a Christian, was sorry for what he had done, and he wanted to plead guilty because he was, in fact, guilty. I told him I was a Christian too, and I invited him to pray with me. Together, we confessed our sins and asked Jesus to forgive us. He was shocked at my approach, but he said again, "I really just want to plead guilty to this thing."

I cautioned him, "Let's just see what the Lord will do for you."

When the day for the court appearance came, I had to hustle to speak to the prosecutor, like all the other attorneys looking for a deal in this very busy urban courtroom. I noticed that when I spoke, the prosecutor began to panic. He excused himself and disappeared for a while. When he came back, he told me with great embarrassment that the file for the case seemed to be missing. He asked me to share my copies with him, but since I was not obligated to do so, I declined.

The prosecutor had to tell the judge in open court that the case had to be dismissed because all the papers — the police report, witness statements (and there were many), complainants reports, and tickets — were nowhere to be found. I had them all in my file, of course, but it was not my duty to disclose them. The judge was forced to agree for all charges against my client to be dropped because there were no incriminating records.

Since it was not clear what had just happened, my client asked me why they had not prosecuted him. I told him that God had indeed forgiven him completely, and he could go home as a free man. He assured me he would never get in trouble with the law again.

That day I saw the truth of Colossians 2:13-14 in action:

> *He has made [you] alive together with Him, having forgiven you all trespasses, having wiped out the handwriting of requirements that was against us, which was contrary to us. And he has taken it out of the way, having nailed it to the cross.*

God has done what we could not do. He has erased all the accusations and recorded sins that stand against us. The requirements of the Law are clearly written, but God has overcome them all, and we are free to go and live our lives in peace!

MIRACLES IN THE MARKETPLACE

Those who go down to the sea in ships,
Who do business on great waters,
They see the works of the LORD,
And His wonders in the deep.
For He commands and raises the stormy wind,
Which lifts up the waves of the sea.
They mount up to the heavens,
They go down again to thew depths;
Their soul melts because of trouble.
They reel to and fro, and stagger like a drunken man,
And are at their wits' end.
Then they cry out to the LORD in their trouble,
And He brings them out of their distresses.
He calms the storm,
So that its waves are still.
Then they are glad because they are quiet;
So He guides them to their desired haven.
Oh that men would give thanks to the LORD for His goodness
And for His wonderful works to the children of men!

Psalm 107:23-31

We could spend our whole lives getting to know Jesus better and still not discover all of His wonderful attributes. It's like looking at a diamond from different angles under different lighting. The various surfaces continue to show different colors and reflections.

Often we hear about the wonderful healings that Jesus performed during His lifetime, and He is still doing that through the prayers of His people. Can we also cry out to Him with our more mundane problems? YES! Absolutely!

These sailors didn't need a healing or a deliverance; they needed the sea to be made calm. Do you need that? Do you have a terrible problem with your family or some other situation that needs God's intervention, an impossible business problem perhaps? If a miracle is needed, Jesus is well able to provide grace in your time of need. As I once heard the well known evangelist Charles Capps say, "Grace is God's willingness to get involved in your situation, even though you don't deserve it."

Jonah found himself in a predicament. He didn't want to obey God and evangelize Nineveh (modern-day Iraq), and so he found himself in the stomach of a great fish with no hope and no apparent way out. Thank God he came to his senses and cried out to God, and God made the fish so uncomfortable that he vomited poor Jonah out on the beach. Jonah apparently broke one of the fish's teeth on the way out because it's on display in a museum in Iraq to this day.

After coming to his senses and while still in the fish, Jonah worshiped God. He said:

When my soul fainted within me,
I remembered the LORD;
And my prayer went up to You,
Into Your holy temple.

Those who regard worthless idols
Forsake their own mercy.
But I will sacrifice to You
With the voice of thanksgiving;
I will pay what I have vowed.
Salvation is of the LORD.   Jonah 2:7-9

"Those who regard worthless idols forsake their own mercy." Allow me to translate. Those who only know religion (worship of a god who doesn't see, hear, or speak) may never know the ups and downs of life like Jonah, but they will also never know the joy and freedom of knowing a God who does miracles. Sometimes Jesus just asks us to get out of the way and let Him do His work.

Once my wife Emily and I were asked to pray for young lady who had a terrible physical deformity. Her back was visibly twisted, and her chin actually touched her chest. The muscles on one side of her neck were massive—like a football player—because all day, every day, she was trying to lift her head. Emily asked her how long she had been in this condition, and she said it had been about ten years, ever since she was a teenager. She had been to many doctors, but there seemed to be no cure. Later we learned that this strange condition actually had a name—torticollis.

When you're sensitive to the Holy Spirit He can lead you in how to minister to those in need. In this case, Emily was led to ask if there might be someone the young lady needed to forgive. In fact, there was. She told us of an man who had taken advantage of her as a fifteen-year-old girl. Emily encouraged her to forgive this man, as hard as that might be. We led her in a prayer of forgiveness and deliverance, and she immediately straightened up and began to pray in the Spirit. Praise God!

This young lady's exuberance and joy were unrestrained, and she danced and laughed so loud that everyone could hear. What joy! A beautiful smile came over her face and was still there when she left those healing rooms.

God is still doing miracles today, and He is still doing them in our daily lives. When we are at our wits end, like those sailors in Psalm 107, and when there is no solution or cure, that is when God comes in and shows us what He alone can do. Those who are stuck in religion never experience the joy and freedom that God provides when

He moves by His strong arm and delivers those of us who cry out for His help.

Aside from our work in the healing rooms, this type of miraculous healing has not been our common experience. Our miracles have occurred more in the realm of wisdom for the daily work in our legal practice.

LET THE HOLY SPIRIT DO HIS WORK

When I was a young man, my family had a house in Massachusetts next to a majestic pine forest. There were hundreds of pine trees covering probably forty acres. The trees stood in rows, very close together, standing about a hundred feet tall. It was an old Christmas tree farm that had been abandoned about thirty years earlier. For me, this forest was a very special, majestic place to walk.

There, in that forest of pines, all of the outside noises were hushed. The lower branches of the trees had long since fallen off, so your eyes were drawn straight up to the tops of the trees where the live branches formed a canopy overhead. We called it "the pine cathedral."

Because pine needles had fallen from these trees for so many years, they formed a soft carpet underfoot, and our feet sank down into them as we walked. For some reason, those Christmas trees had been left to grow to their full height.

Isaiah 32:15-17 says:

LET THE HOLY SPIRIT DO HIS WORK

Until the Spirit is poured upon us from on high,
And the wilderness becomes a fruitful field,
And the fruitful field is counted as a forest.
Then justice will dwell in the wilderness,
And righteousness remain in the fruitful field.
The work of righteousness will be peace,
And the effect of righteousness, quietness and assurance
forever.

This is the way Isaiah described a series of events which transform life through the outpouring of God's Spirit. First:

Until the Spirit is poured upon us from on high,
And the wilderness becomes a fruitful field,

When it rains in the desert, vegetation seems to spring up from nothing in just a few days. You'll see blossoms and young shoots almost immediately. When the Holy Spirit is poured out, He produces salvation, new birth, and He brings new life to dry believers right away. This is exciting and important, but the Holy Spirit doesn't want us to stop there. He doesn't want to produce temporary blossoms that survive only a few days.

The third line of this passage says, *"The fruitful field is counted as a forest,"* or *"the fertile field seems like a forest."* The rain continues for years until the fertile field grows so dramatically that it actually becomes a forest. The field never stops growing. A fragile young tree eventually becomes a mighty oak. This represents long-term sustained growth. The Holy Spirit wants to pour Himself out in our lives for years and years, long enough to really change us, long enough to touch deep areas of our lives and keep on doing so, long enough to produce spiritual maturity.

For our part, we must cooperate with this work. If we stick with it, He's bound to change us. We need to allow Him to point things out, convicting us of things we have to change, and bringing about spiritual maturity. He wants to grow us to *"the measure of the stature of the fullness of Christ"* (Ephesians 4:13). He will not be satisfied until He produces some very tall oak trees.

What does a person look like when he or she has allowed this kind of growth to take place over years? What does the full-grown tree look like? We need to look at the Old Testament to see examples of some such tall trees. Daniel is a great example.

We know Daniel as an intercessor who kept asking God for more. The Holy Spirit began to work in this man when he was just a teenager and worked wisdom, practical knowledge, administration, and other gifts into him over many years of preparation. The Bible says of Daniel: *"They could find no corruption in him, because he was trustworthy and neither corrupt nor negligent"* (Daniel 6:4, NIV).

Daniel could also solve difficult problems. As an adult, he was trusted to prophesy and interpret dreams for the rulers of the nation of Babylon. When the Holy Spirit worked in this man's life, it impacted an entire nation. Because of this, Daniel became head administrator under three kings—Nebuchadnezzar, Belshazzar, and Darius. During the reign of the third king, probably late in Daniel's life, he was still pressing God for more. He had read Jeremiah's prophecy about Jerusalem and about the timing of the end of the Babylonian captivity, and he set his heart to intercede for the nation. He fasted for twenty-one days, repenting for the sins of his people and pleading with God for their deliverance.

In response, God gave Daniel a vision of what would take place in the nation of Israel. Daniel still kept asking for more, and God showed him about the coming of the Messiah. He asked for more again, and God showed him about the Church in the last days (the forest I'm talking about). God also showed him about the last days themselves. In all three of the administrations he served, circumstances were worked through him which compelled the rulers he served under to acknowledge that the God of Israel was the one true God.

On the one hand, Daniel was comfortable running a secular country, and on the other hand, he would have participated in our twenty-first century church meetings.

There isn't time or space to say much about the other Old Testament giants of faith. David had a gift of prophetic song and became king over Israel. Joseph could interpret dreams, and the Pharaoh in Egypt turned over the administration of the entire kingdom to him. Miriam prophesied and led the nation in singing and dancing. Deborah was a prophetess and warrior who became a judge.

Having one Daniel impacted a nation. What if God had produced an entire nation of Daniels, Davids, Deborahs, Josephs, and Miriams? What if God had produced an entire forest of such trees? He said:

Then justice will dwell in the wilderness,
And righteousness remain in the fruitful field.

The Holy Spirit wants to create a whole new environment, an environment where justice and righteousness can dwell. He wants to prepare His Church for the coming of the righteous King.

When the Holy Spirit is allowed to work, He brings about righteousness and justice. We need to let the Holy Spirit work with us long enough for Him to address things that need to be addressed.

Once, about thirty years ago, while I was jogging in the city where I lived, the Lord said to me, "WE HAVE NOTHING IN COMMON." This hit me like a ton of bricks. Since God doesn't change, guess who needed to. This was just one of many times the Lord confronted me. Let Him point out some areas in you that need to change. The process of repentance can be painful, and it even feels like death (a death to self), but let Him complete His work.

In many places where the Scriptures mention the coming of the Messiah and the outpouring of the Holy Spirit, you will notice that in next breath, the Word refers to the bringing about of *justice:*

> *Behold! My Servant whom I uphold,*
> *My Elect One in whom My soul delights!*
> *I have put My Spirit upon Him;*
> *He will bring forth justice to the Gentiles.*
> *He will not cry out, nor raise His voice,*
> *Nor cause His voice to be heard in the street.*
> *A bruised reed He will not break,*
> *And smoking flax He will not quench;*
> *He will bring forth justice for truth.*
> *He will not fail nor be discouraged,*
> *Till He has established justice in the earth;*
> *And the coastlands shall wait for His law.*
>
> Isaiah 42:1-4

The Holy Spirit brings about justice. Justice is righteousness on a governmental scale. What if God were to place many Daniels in our government? Would that change things? When there is one Daniel in a nation, that nation is impacted. When there is one tree, we admire the tree, but when there is an entire forest of trees, an entirely new environment is created. When we have many Daniels, Miriams, Davids, and Deborahs, society is changed.

I believe the Holy Spirit wants to create a whole new environment in the Church today. His Church is majestic, mature, and stable, and He wants to continue to pour Himself out until this forest is completely matured. The Holy Spirit is doing something deeper, something lasting, something more. Let Him do His work.

I think the Holy Spirit wants to grow an entire majestic forest of these tall trees. We are often satisfied with little Christmas trees. Can you imagine how upset you would be if you owned a forest and your intention was to grow the forest to its maturity, but person after person stopped by to cut down and remove a tree? If each one cut a tree that stood five to six feet tall, took it home to put it on display for a couple of weeks at Christmas time, and then threw it away, how would you feel?

Some people think that going forward for prayer once or twice in church is all the Holy Spirit wants us to do. As wonderful as that is, it's not "one and done" or a mere experience to be enjoyed. A person may say, "This is all the Holy Spirit wants to do. I don't need to seek Him anymore. Let's see what else life has to offer." By saying this, we cut down the tree, and that's the end of it. Instead, the

Holy Spirit wants to do more and more in our lives until we reach spiritual maturity.

A mature forest is stable. Adolescent forests are changeable and very susceptible to wind, storms, and the elements. But a mature forest can endure almost anything. I went back to the pine forest a few weeks ago. The house is gone, except for a piece of the foundation, but the pine cathedral is about the same as before, still standing straight and tall. The tree trunks are a little thicker, but the forest is intact. God said:

Then justice will dwell in the wilderness,
And righteousness remain in the fruitful field.

What is the effect of righteousness?
The work of righteousness will be peace,
And the effect of righteousness, quietness and assurance forever.

The natural effect of righteousness is peace. There is a benefit to going through all the pain. God wants to take us to the place where we can experience His peace. If He is doing something unsettling in our lives, it may mean that He has something more to show us. He brings up some problems to force us to go forward to discover more about Him. He gives us the promise of quietness and confidence, stability in the midst of instability.

You very often cannot imagine what the end result of a thing will be. When you're standing in the desert, you can't imagine that same location as a thriving forest. In the very same way, you can't imagine what your life will look like after the Holy Spirit has done His work in you over years and years or what the Lord wants to accomplish through you or through the Church as a whole. Sometimes we can't imagine our lives being full of quietness and confidence, but that is God's promise.

That time in church when you went forward for prayer was an introduction to a Person rather than a temporary experience. He is a very real Person, and just as He did through Daniel, He can speak to you throughout life. This is just the introduction to the Holy Spirit who wants to change deep areas in our lives. He wants to bring spiritual maturity, righteousness, justice, peace, confidence, quietness, security, and stability in the midst of instability.

Have we arrived yet? Has the Church arrived? No, but the Holy Spirit is the Person who can change us. If you haven't met Him yet, I'd like to introduce you to Him today.

WHERE'S THE FRUIT?

When I was at Princeton in the 1970s during the Jesus People Movement, I thought that all of us were called to the same thing—to go out two by two and preach the Gospel. In fact, that is what we did, visiting various students two by two. We wore sandals and had long hair and straggly, poor excuses for beards, but our work never produced any fruit. It never occurred to us that God might not be working that same way anymore. That method may indeed have been appropriate for others or for a certain time, but it didn't work for us. Jesus always does things in new ways, and He has unique roles for each person. He said:

> *You did not choose Me, but I chose you and appointed you that you should go and bear fruit, and that your fruit should remain, that whatever you ask the Father in My name He may give you.*   John 15:16

God is like a Great Administrator who assigns tasks to His people. Each task fits the individual person perfectly.

I thought He assigned each of us the same task, but He doesn't say that. John 15:16 just says, *"And that your fruit should remain."* Remain here means "last."

When I was in high school, I had just gotten saved and started Bible studies and meetings with other students. I was zealous but completely ineffective and very annoying. There was no lasting fruit. Where do you see effectiveness and lasting fruit in your life? This may be evidence of the role that God has destined for you.

I would not be a successful kindergarten teacher. There's no telling where the children would end up, probably playing in the middle of a busy street. Jesus put a high value on working with and protecting children, even to just giving them a cup of water. He said this would be rewarded (see Matthew 10:42). He also put a high value on protecting children from harm. I could give them a cup of cold water, but working with them every day? Probably not.

At first, I was disappointed that the Lord had not called me to a pulpit ministry, but after many years, the Holy Spirit showed me this scripture:

> *Pure and undefiled religion before God and the Father is this: to visit orphans and widows in their trouble, and to keep oneself unspotted from the world.*   James 1:27

In Bible times, the men would often die young, leaving widows and children to fend for themselves. They needed the help of God's people. Today, the Lord showed me, those who most need our attention are not just widows and orphans, but older couples who are destitute and vulnerable. They very often fall prey to so-called "financial advisors" who take their money through sketchy schemes. Our elderly are even vulnerable to their own children who, too often, take advantage of them and abuse them. They are also vulnerable to the poor care given by some nursing homes. The modern translation of that verse for me is:

> *True religion is working with and protecting the elderly who are vulnerable.*

This is what I do for a living—estate planning to protect the savings of the elderly for generations to come, providing financial solutions to pay for assisted living and skilled care when necessary, and reducing estate taxes. Over the years I've worked with thousands of couples, most of whom would never have darkened the doors of a church.

The modern translation of James 1:27 for you may be different but just as powerful, for instance:

> *True religion is raising children who love Jesus in a world that has forgotten Him.*

The work of the Holy Spirit through God's people must not be limited.

I was once asked to prophesy over some Princeton students in a small fellowship. While prophesying over one young man, I saw that he was a mathematician or physicist and that the Lord would allow him to think "outside the box." He would be given mathematical solutions that others had not yet seen. The Holy Spirit would give him gifts in this area just as He gives gifts of knowledge or wisdom to others for their chosen work. This man's type of work would be honored and developed by the Holy Spirit to increase the Kingdom. As it turned out, the young man had been thinking about giving up his plans associated with math and physics to go to Bible school. This word from God kept him on course. I've found that the Holy Spirit gives workday solutions to scholars, businesspeople, and workers of every stripe, and He gives us fruit.

Another time I was asked to prophesy over various people in a congregation, and when I prayed for a particular lady, I saw her serving lunches to children in a cafeteria. The strange thing was that I saw her dressed in royal robes and imparting the Holy Spirit to those she served. It turned out that she was indeed a cafeteria worker at an elementary school, and every day she dished out food for children on the cafeteria line. What an encouragement this was to her that her job was anointed and a blessing to the children she served! Her version of James 1:27 might be:

True religion is serving healthy food to ungrateful children.

Solomon had a different call than his father. David had been a warrior all his life. He, together with his mighty men, had conquered all the territory of ancient Israel. He and his people had lived in tents all their lives, travelling whenever they needed to. Imagine young Solomon's concern when his father turned over the kingdom to him! He now had a large number of restive people to govern, as well as the task of building the first Temple for Almighty God according to certain exacting specifications.

In the face of this overwhelming task, Solomon asked God for wisdom in a dream. Through the supernatural gift of wisdom imparted to him, great things were accomplished. Here are just a few examples:

- Solomon created a labor force.
- He engineered brand new building systems.
- He kept a standing army.
- He created a taxing system.
- He gathered gifted craftsmen and artisans for the Temple construction.

- He built houses for himself and also for his father, King David.
- He traded with neighboring kings for supplies.

The Temple Solomon built was one of the seven wonders of the ancient world, and some aspects of its construction are still a mystery today. This was the result of the *"word of wisdom"* described in 1 Corinthians 12:8 deposited in one man. What might we accomplish if God gave us all this gift of wisdom?

Solomon entered into a new era, and he brought his people in with him. Instead of conquering lands like his father, he enjoyed peace, stability, and wealth. People came from far and wide just to hear his wisdom. Even the Queen of Sheba traveled to Jerusalem to hear his words. It was a new era of honor for Israel spearheaded by gifts and callings that God had given to Solomon. How will God change the dynamic for the Church in this new era we find ourselves in today? Where is the fruit?

"Words Will Be As Cheap As Water"

In recent years, the Holy Spirit spoke to me and said, "Words will be as cheap as water." With the introduction of artificial intelligence (AI) and the advancements of the internet, words are no longer just within the authority of man, but are now written and spoken by machines. All the more reason to inquire of the Holy Spirit for His wisdom, which will never be overridden by machines. All the more reason to operate in the character and power of God the Holy Spirit.

When Jesus was tempted in the wilderness, He responded in both the character of maturity and in the wisdom given to Him by the Holy Spirit for the moment. He had all the power of God at His disposal in the Holy Spirit, but it was His character that said "NO! I will not turn this rock into bread because *'Man shall not live by bread alone'*" (Matthew 4:4). The Holy Spirit was present and living in Him, but it was His character that won the battle. He did not have what we have, death to the old nature through the blood of the cross. He stood against the enemy based only on His own sinless nature and holiness. It's time for the Church to wake up to a new era!

One day, as I was walking into church from the parking lot, someone slapped me on the back of my head, and the impact was so great I almost fell over. I heard the word of the Lord say, "It's time for the Church to wake up!" I looked around, but there was no one there. This was God's doing. It's time to change the game, to get ahead of it, time to change the way church is done. It's a new era!

When Guttenberg invented the printing press in the 1500s, the first thing he printed was the Bible. Little did he know that by putting the Word of God into the hands of ordinary people in their language, a revolution would take place. When people were able to read, along with Martin Luther, that they could be saved simply by faith rather than through works and paying money to the church, it brought about a total reformation. Faith entered into them by the simple reading of the Word.

Similarly, through the internet, a great revolution is now taking place. The Word of God is available all over the world, even in the most remote locations on earth in the language of the people. Worldwide evangelism is the result, and it is happening because of the dissemination of the Word of God. This is a revolution that will be greater than the Great Reformation brought about by Martin Luther.

Your Work Shall Be Rewarded

Azariah, the son of the prophet Obed, prophesied to King Asa:

And he went out to meet Asa, and said to him: "Hear me, Asa, and all Judah and Benjamin. The LORD is with you while you are with Him. If you seek Him, He will be found by you; but if you forsake Him, He will forsake you. For a long time Israel has been without the true God, without a teaching priest, and without law; but when in their trouble they turned to the LORD God of Israel, and sought Him, He was found by them. And in those times there was no peace to the one who went out, nor to the one who came in, but great turmoil was on all the inhabitants of the lands. So nation was destroyed by nation, and city by city, for God troubled them with every adversity. BUT YOU, BE STRONG AND DO NOT LET YOUR HANDS BE WEAK, FOR YOUR WORK SHALL BE REWARDED!"

2 Chronicles 15:2-7, Emphasis Mine

King Asa took these words to heart and embarked on a new path for Israel. He led the people on a journey of repentance. They removed all the idols in the land and restored the altar of the Lord. They gathered in what we might call a multi-day regional conference and made offerings to the Lord. Next, they *"entered into a covenant to seek the LORD God of their fathers with all their heart and with all their soul"* (2 Chronicles 15:12). As an answer to their earnest prayers and hard work, God *"gave them rest all around"* (verse 15).

This promise of God to reward hard work also appears in Jeremiah 31:16:

Thus says the LORD:
"Refrain your voice from weeping,
And your eyes from tears;
For YOUR WORK SHALL BE REWARDED, *says the LORD,*
And they shall come back from the land of the enemy.
(Emphasis Mine)

Jesus chose hard workers when He chose His disciples. Peter and his companion fishermen had *"toiled all night"* (Luke 5:5). They were not simply casting out a line; they were hauling large heavy nets made even heavier when wet. Peter said, *"Master, we have toiled all night and caught nothing; nevertheless at Your word I will let down the net"* (same verse). These were hardworking men.

In my own law practice, there have been many difficult times. I distinctly remember going to the grocery store, picking out a full week's groceries and handing the food to the lady at check-out counter, but when I attempted to use my credit cards, I found they were all maxed-out. I had to leave the bags at the counter and walk out empty-handed.

I've had to learn what it means to "work hard." I never had to learn that lesson as a student or as someone else's employee. Even this year in the practice, we have been so overwhelmed with new business that my wife and I have had to work seven days a week. It has been the most difficult thing we have ever had to do. Even at our age, we are now working harder than ever.

Emily and I were privileged to join a missionary couple in the Dominican Republic to minister to their church in one of the most remote areas of that country. We could see the discouragement and disheartenment on the faces of the people. This scripture came to me to preach from 2 Chronicles 15:2: *"YOUR WORK SHALL BE REWARDED!"* I said, "We all know people who have worked hard but never saw a reward. But God has given us a promise that if we work hard, we will see the reward of our work! This is His promise."

There was a large group of children and young people in the congregation, and I asked them to repeat after me.

"MY STUDIES WILL BE REWARDED!" and "MY WORK IN CLASS WILL BE REWARDED!" This promise is from the Father, and it's good regardless of our current circumstances. I believe some of those children (and also some of the adults) received that word.

Emily and I were invited to call out people in the congregation to prophesy over them. Emily, in her boldness, asked a couple to stand up. She then said to the man, "God is doing a work in you. You will have meetings in your home, and many people will come."

At this point, the pastor interrupted us and asked the man if he had invited Jesus into his life (knowing that he had not). The man accepted the Lord right then and there. We later learned that he had the biggest and most expensive house in the whole village because he was a drug dealer. But now, it seemed, his beautiful house would be used for Jesus' meetings! Glory to God!

During one downtown meeting in the Dominican Republic, the Holy Spirit took me to Heaven to look down on the church. I saw a signpost announcing that this location in the Dominican Republic was marked for revival. I saw angels standing in a row to the right and the left holding a net which stretched between them. They looked at us as if they were waiting for us to do something.

Indeed, they were waiting for us, and the Lord asked, "Are you ready for the harvest? Will you work with Me for harvest? The angels are waiting, and they will gather it. It does not matter if you are assigned to preach, teach, take care of children, or sweep the floor. Will you gather with Me?" We have since learned that the church building was completed, and that area has indeed experienced a great revival.

In the New Testament, Stephen was chosen to serve widows. He was a waiter, and yet as he entered into this work, he enjoyed the favor, miracles, and glory of God. Martha served the disciples and was mildly chided by Jesus for worrying too much about preparing the food, but Jesus didn't tell Martha to stop doing what she was doing; He just told her to stop fussing. The Lord never told people *not* to work, but He wants us to put our work in perspective. Note that it was Martha, not Mary, who had the testimony when she met Jesus after Lazarus died. She said to Him, *"Yes, Lord, I believe that You are the Christ, the Son of God, who is to come into the world"* (John 11:27).

Does a person who works in the world receive a lesser reward than a preacher called to preach? Absolutely not (seeEphesians 6:7-8)! If a man or woman is called to preach, then they should preach. But if a man or woman is not called to preach but to work in the world or keep the home, he or she will be more blessed in that service. As John the Baptist showed us, any man or woman only has what he or she receives from Heaven (see John 3:27). But whatever we do, Jesus sees and honors our hard work (see Revelation 2:2).

MIRACLES IN THE MARKETPLACE

One of the revivalists and preachers of the Great Reformation, John Witherspoon, accepted a position as President of Princeton University. He said he wanted to train up "students in the nation's service." He wanted to prepare them to bring revival and reformation. The University has long since lost its roots, but the principle John Witherspoon put forth remains the same. God continues to use men and women who are willing to spread the fragrance of His presence in every area of life.

Once, when praying for a small group of students at Princeton, the word of the Lord came to me for them:

> "You are the church of the diaspora. You will soon go your separate ways [they were not training for professional ministry]. For a few years you will keep your branding iron in the hot coals of the worship at the Princeton meetings, and then you will take that iron and put My brand on all the companies and organizations you go to."

Yes, your work will be rewarded, so find your field of service.

CAN A CHRISTIAN BE A LAWYER?

My little children, these things I write to you, so that you may not sin. And if anyone sins, we have an Advocate with the Father, Jesus Christ the righteous. 1 John 2:1

When I first realized that God had not called me to be a pastor, I worked with lawyers at the State Legislature on a study commission investigating fraud in nursing homes and decided that I could do legal work. But many friends confronted me, insisting that a Christian could never be a lawyer, not a true Christian anyway, only someone who was compromised. Were they right? As you can see in 1 John 2:1, Jesus Himself is called our Advocate. If Christians cannot be lawyers, our Legislature, largely comprised of lawyers, would be devoid of believers.

Despite all the arguments, I felt that I could serve God as a lawyer, and this has proven true. Jesus often confronts me with new areas of the law to learn, shows me how to avoid mistakes, and reminds me of things I have failed to do in a given case. He gives me a strategy for each case and reminds me to reach out to clients who may need to update their estate planning. He even reminds me to send out mass mailings to generate new business. He is truly my Senior Partner.

God often gives me unique answers in a case that I would never have thought of. For example, He has shown me ways to describe complex tax issues with simple diagrams. He even provides unique billing solutions, corrects me on unintended billing errors. He said:

Call to Me, and I will answer you, and show you great and mighty things, which you do not know.
Jeremiah 33:3

Let me give you another example of the unique solutions God gives:

A client approached me with an unusual and difficult problem. His grandfather, a well-liked Princeton American History professor, had built a house in 1909 right in Princeton, and when he died, he left the house to his wife. She had a fondness for her grandson, my client, and also a deep attachment to the town of Princeton. As a result, in her Will she granted her grandson a "life estate" in the house. That meant he could stay there for the rest of his life without rent. Then, upon his death, the house would go to his niece for the rest of her life, and then finally, after both had died, it would revert to Princeton University.

Can a Christian Be a Lawyer?

At the time my client approached me, he was about sixty-five and had lived in this house for many years already. He could no longer afford the high property taxes in town,[1] and his niece never wanted to return to Princeton for any reason.

For his part, my client desperately wanted to move out West, where his ailing wife could enjoy better health. If he simply listed the house for sale and took all the proceeds for himself, the University could sue him for the value of their remainder interest. He approached me to try to sell his interest to the University and get him out from under that burden.

I was not the first lawyer to work on this case. My client had used two other attorneys to go to court on his behalf in an attempt to compel the University to buy the house, but in both cases, the judge refused to force the University to do that. As result, the man was stuck. He couldn't afford the taxes, and he didn't have enough money to move.

I approached the University to offer to sell my client's "life estate interest" to them, and they almost went along with it, even to the point of reviewing and almost accepting the contract I presented. But, at the very last minute, they decided against it. They had many other properties, and they didn't want to add this house, which they considered an "eye-sore," to their portfolio. No professor would want to live there. So, we were stalemated.

---

1. $24,000 a year

Then I got an idea, which I believe came from the Lord: Why not turn the whole proposal on its head? I approached the University from a totally different angle. "Let's enter into a contract," I proposed, "to permit my client to sell the property on the open market, but agree to preserve the niece's interest as well as the University's remaining interest and split the proceeds according to the life estate tables generated by the IRS — the value presumed after both life estates had ended." In that way, my client would be free, and the University would not have to take over the improvement of the house. The University was gracious about it and agreed in principle.

After lengthy negotiations, proposals, competing appraisals and contracts, the real estate agents were able to sell the house, my client was able to receive enough to buy a house elsewhere, and God got all the glory! That tactic set this couple free after being locked into living in that house for decades in a place they couldn't afford and in a town where they couldn't even get a job. Jesus gets all the glory.

When the Pharisees confronted Jesus about His disciples picking corn on the Sabbath, He defended His guys. (Have you ever been accused by religious folks on a picky thing they thought was "ungodly"? I have!)

I don't know the rules of the day about picking corn on the Sabbath, but it must have been illegal. Jesus reminded the Pharisees of a precedent, a lot like a lawyer would do today. He reminded them of David eating the "showbread" from the Temple without being condemned for doing so (see 1 Samuel 21:1-6). I'm sure that eating the showbread was far worse than eating corn on the Sabbath!

Even though His disciples had been caught dead to rights, Jesus found a way to defend them. This is the work of a creative lawyer. In the same way, we can find God's mercy and forgiveness. He defends us today when we are accused, and He is our Advocate even when we have no one else defending us.

When the Pharisees asked, "Should we pay taxes to Caesar?" Jesus asked for a coin, and with a brilliant piece of lawyering, He said: "Whose image is on it?"

"Caesar's" they replied.

Jesus' conclusion was:

Render therefore to Caesar the things that are Caesar's, and to God the things that are God's. Matthew 22:21

No one could gainsay this comment, and they left Him. His answer was a positive statement of our responsibility to both God and man that no one could question.

Jesus defended the woman caught in adultery with a similar piece of lawyering. While the punishment for that act would have been death by stoning, He wrote on the ground something in the sight of the Pharisees. I imagine He wrote their sins, which were probably also punishable by death: breaking the Sabbath, the sin of pride, making false accusations against a neighbor, etc. Then He said, *"He who is without sin among you, let him throw a stone at her first"* (John 8:7). No one stepped forward. In fact, one by one, they all slipped away.

Then our wonderful Jesus, the Son of God, said something which resounds down through the centuries:

> *When Jesus had raised Himself up and saw no one but the woman, He said to her, "Woman, where are those accusers of yours? Has no one condemned you?"*
> *She said, "No one, Lord."*
> *And Jesus said to her, "Neither do I condemn you; go and sin no more."* John 8:10-11

Forgiveness of sin from Jesus is always the way to start a new life of freedom. Therefore a believing lawyer can work with Jesus as his Senior Partner to represent clients.

Jesus Dealt with the Sin Problem

Several years ago, I met with a client who wanted to bring a lawsuit. He had been clearly wronged and had lost money as a result. It was a good case, so I took him on as a client. He puffed out his chest and said he would litigate "for the principle of the thing!" He also paid my retainer, which is always a good sign of commitment.

To my new client, who was a believer, this was a battle of good versus evil, right versus wrong. It was right up there with Elijah confronting the prophets of Baal in the Bible. Just think about the pressure this put on me as his attorney! Now I had to succeed because God's reputation was on the line!

My client said he had done everything right, and I believed him. But litigation is a long process. It's not a single battle, but a series of smaller engagements.

My adversary asked for the "production of documents," and he took depositions of my clients, which is normal. I also took depositions, asked for documents, and propounded interrogatories on the other side.

Even after the discovery process, our case was excellent. Then, however, the opposing attorney found one small thing that my client had failed to do. (I don't recall the details, but they're not relevant). Everyone makes mistakes, but if a mistake is "immaterial," it will not impact the outcome, and that was the case here. The vast majority of the facts were in our favor, and the case would be won.

Nevertheless, my client was crestfallen at the exposure of his mistake, and he collapsed like a house of cards. Because his single mistake was exposed, he could not stand it. Even though I tried to convince him to proceed, he asked, even begged me, to settle the case. He had no courage left.

Jesus wants men and women of courage who will prevail, not based upon their own righteousness, which is illusory. He wants us to prevail with courage based on His righteousness. If we rely on our own ability to "do everything right," we are scared, timid, weak and live a life of limitation dictated by our fears and the judgments that others place on us.

A biblical personality who relied on his ability to do everything right was Job. Indeed, the Bible says he was *"blameless."*

> *Have you considered My servant Job, that there is none like him on the earth, a blameless and upright man, one who fears God and shuns evil?* Job 1:8

Jesus Dealt with the Sin Problem

The issue was not righteousness with God. Having gained it, Job still didn't "get it."

The older brother of the Prodigal Son didn't get it either. He had remained faithful to his father while his brother squandered his inheritance in riotous living. The thing God wants is relationship, not someone trying to do everything right. He wants total abandonment, with faith in the depth of His loving relationship with us and a confidence that He is with us.

By contrast, Job was always afraid — afraid he would lose his good standing with the Father by slipping up. He thought he had succeeded in business because he followed all the rules. However, the faith in his relationship with God, which he gained in the end — the faith in God's priorities — set him free from his religion of fear.

God's will is not us trying to do the right thing, but living in abandonment, living in freedom in Him. He wants relationships with grown-up people, people who know what to do and do it, people who no longer need child training, or need to be held all the time, or who need to be told what to do. He wants men and women who know His ways and walk in them, no longer worrying about missing the mark. Jesus has dealt with the sin problem once and for all, so live free in Him.

Continuous Blessing

When I realized that I was not called to be a pastor, I was disappointed at first, but over time I came to the realization that the work of the Holy Spirit is for everyone in society, not just the preachers. He is for all of us, no matter what our profession may be.

When I got saved, the Holy Spirit was never mentioned. He was the uncle you didn't want to invite to Thanksgiving. You didn't understand Him and didn't want to get to know Him. He might lead you down a path of fanaticism or emotionalism, so you couldn't trust Him. I was like the men in Acts who said they didn't even know there was a Holy Spirit (see Acts 19:2).

But there IS a Holy Spirit, and Jesus spent a great deal of time describing Him and the work He would do (see, for instance, John 14-16). He said the Holy Spirit would be a Comforter and a Teacher. He would show us the future. He would take everything that Jesus had said and done and give it to us. He would give us words when we needed them.

If we look at Ezekiel 47, we see that the Spirit only does good things. This is a picture of the reformation of all of society to be brought about by the Holy Spirit:

Then he brought me back to the door of the temple; and there was water, flowing from under the threshold of the temple toward the east, for the front of the temple faced east; the water was flowing from under the right side of the temple, south of the altar. He brought me out by way of the north gate and led me around on the outside to the outer gateway that faces east; and there was water, running out on the right side.

And when the man went out to the east with the line in his hand, he measured one thousand cubits, and he brought me through the waters; the water came up to my ankles. Again he measured one thousand and brought me through the waters; the water came up to my knees. Again, he measured one thousand and brought me through; the water came up to my waist. Again he measured one thousand, and it was a river that I could not cross; for the water was too deep, water in which one must swim, a river that could not be crossed. He said to me, "Son of man, have you seen this?" Then he brought me and returned me to the bank of the river.

When I returned, there, along the bank of the river, were very many trees on one side and the other.

Ezekiel 47:1-7

The Holy Spirit changes structures, changes seasons, and brings life to dead things in the most unlikely places. The Holy Spirit, like this river, brings life wherever He goes. He changes things. He cleans up the murky water made foul by sin and transforms it so it will hold life. In other words, He cleans up our lives.

One day I sensed there was something wrong in my relationship with the Lord. Can you tell when there's something wrong in one of your relationships? Your wife is unusually silent. She's hurt. Or a friend has not been in touch for a long time, and you start to speculate about what the problem might be. Finally, you humble yourself and ask, "What's wrong?" The Lord is not obliged to tell you. You have to ask (see Luke 11:9), but if you ask humbly and persistently like a friend, He will tell you.

I asked one day because I sensed there was something wrong. Had I failed to pay a bill? Had I missed a tithe? Did I have an overdue library book? But none of these things seemed to hit the mark.

I had just completed a job with the State Legislature at the Nursing Home Study Commission, investigating fraud, and as a benefit for being a part of this I was given a train pass that allowed me free passage on any trains in the State for a year. Even though I was no longer an employee, I was using the pass to travel by train to law school. I suddenly realized this was a sin, and as soon as I bought my own monthly ticket, I was free again. God's joy returned.

Buying that ticket was painful to do because it cost $60 a month at a time when I was working several jobs to make my way through law school, but I was so glad I had obeyed.

Ezekiel continues:

Then he said to me: "This water flows toward the eastern region, goes down into the valley, and enters the sea. When it reaches the sea, its waters are healed."

Ezekiel 47:8

There was so much water that it changed the environment. As God's Spirit flows, the worst, most corrupt places become clean and healthy, and this provision is for all of society. It brings a time of reformation.

The next verse declares:

And it shall be that every living thing that moves, wherever the rivers go, will live. Ezekiel 47:9

In fact, we are the temple of the Holy Spirit. Wherever we go things happen, for the Holy Spirit brings life wherever He goes, and He now lives in us. Our every work is now blessed (see Psalm 1). We just have to choose to let Him work through us.

Verse 9 concludes:

> *There will be a very great multitude of fish, because these waters go there; for they will be healed, and everything will live wherever the river goes.*

Yes, the Holy Spirit transforms the most unlikely places and makes the things of God easy:

> *It shall be that fishermen will stand by it from En Gedi to En Eglaim; they will be places for spreading their nets. Their fish will be of the same kinds as the fish of the Great Sea, exceedingly many.* Ezekiel 47:10

Everywhere this water flows becomes clean, and new life is produced. Fishermen will have great success because of the abundance of fish.

Good fishermen don't stay long in a river that isn't producing. They seek out good places to fish and tell their friends about the best spots. If you allow the Holy Spirit to clean up your business, good businessmen and women will seek you out and tell their friends about you. They're all looking for good fishing holes.

In the most unlikely places, the Holy Spirit provides down-to-earth practical answers and provisions. If we let Him, He will get involved in our business and make it a place for spreading nets, a planned provision. None of this is other-worldly or spooky. This is what God does.

Wherever the Spirit goes, He brings healing, provision, and miracles. He brings good business. He brings prosperity to the marketplace. Business will come to you because of the Holy Spirit, not because of the internet traffic, or blogs, or mass emails, although these things are all good. It is because of the Holy Spirit.

The greatest resource you have is in the Holy Spirit, but your customers and clients may not understand. They just want good fishing, a resource for answers. This is what a good successful business is — a resource, and your clients are experts at finding good resources.

God's Spirit gives life to us wherever we go so we can give life to others — abundant life.

Ezekiel 47:11 declares:

But its swamps and marshes will not be healed; they will be given over to salt.

The Holy Spirit affects all of society and the environment. In Him, there are diverse blessings even in the most unlikely places. Society is not uniform, and who understands that better than God's Spirit?

Along the bank of the river, on this side and that, will grow all kinds of trees used for food; their leaves will not wither, and their fruit will not fail. They will bear fruit every month, because their water flows from the sanctuary. Ezekiel 47:12

Miracles in the Marketplace

The blessings of the Holy Spirit won't fade or disappear. He provides consistent and regular—continuous—blessing and growth, and there is no off season with Him. When I started my practice, it seemed like the worst possible time, but God knows how to bless us despite appearances.

In some places in Vietnam, farmers rely on a single annual crop—rice. If the rains don't come at the right time, they come too late, or there's a monsoon, the rice crop fails, and the farmers lose everything. This is not the case with the Holy Spirit. He provides continuous blessings.

Ezekiel 47:12 concludes:

> *They will bear fruit every month, because their water flows from the sanctuary.*

God's Spirit is a Source of living water from outside of ourselves. It comes from the throne of God, from the cross. We don't have to generate it ourselves. God's Spirit comes inside of us and fills our deepest parts, so that, as the Scriptures say:

> *He who believes in Me, as the Scripture has said, out of his heart will flow rivers of living water.* John 7:38

As we continue to press into God, His Spirit will continue to fill us with more and more of Himself, and all that we touch will be blessed.

Elijah's Restoration
A Practical Path to Good Emotional Health

Elijah had just finished calling down fire on the altar as described in 1 Kings 18, proving to all in Israel that God was the true God and Baal was false. It was a great victory, the likes of which was never again to be seen. However, Jezebel now threatened to kill the prophet, just as she had killed many other prophets of God. Naturally, Elijah was afraid, and he ran for his life. The Bible says:

> *But he himself went a day's journey into the wilderness, and came and sat down under a broom tree. And he prayed that he might die, and said, "It is enough! Now, LORD, take my life, for I am no better than my fathers!"*
>
> 1 Kings 19:4

In answer to this plea, the Lord gently took Elijah through some very natural steps to restore him. I once read a *Reader's Digest* article about what practical steps we should take for good mental health—how we need to combat those bad feelings we all get sometimes. Interestingly, Father God took Elijah through these same steps:

> *Then as he lay and slept under a broom tree, suddenly an angel touched him, and said to him, "Arise and eat." Then he looked, and there by his head was a cake baked on coals, and a jar of water. So he ate and drank, and lay down again. And the angel of the LORD came back the second time, and touched him, and said, "Arise and eat, because the journey is too great for you." So he arose, and ate and drank; and he went in the strength of that food forty days and forty nights as far as Horeb, the mountain of God.*
>
> 1 Kings 19:5-8

GOOD SLEEP: In verse 5, it says, *"then as he lay and slept."* The first recommendation is to get enough sleep every day.

GOOD NUTRITION: In verses 5 and 6, an angel told Elijah to get up and eat, and the necessary food was provided, *"So he ate and drank, and lay down again."* Make sure you get enough healthy food and water.

GOOD EXERCISE: Verse 8 says, *"So he arose, and ate and drank; and he went in the strength of that food forty days and forty nights as far as Horeb, the mountain of God."* The *Reader's Digest* article said that good exercise was the next step toward good mental health. Interestingly, it said that good exercise without proper sleep and without good nutrition is useless.

BE REAL WITH GOD: 1 Kings 19:14 records, *"And he said, 'I have been very zealous for the LORD God of hosts; because the children of Israel have forsaken Your covenant, torn down Your altars, and killed Your prophets with the sword. I alone am left; and they seek to take my life.'"* Although this was never mentioned in the article, I've found that being real with God is important to good health of every kind. Elijah was finally being real and opening up his heart to the Father about his problems and complaints. We should never cover up our feelings, but release them to God. Other people may not be able to handle the depth of our feelings, but God is more than able. The Scriptures declare:

> *Behold, God is mighty, but despises no one;*
> *He is mighty in strength of understanding [heart].*
> Job 36:5

GOOD FRIENDS: In verse 16, the Lord gave Elijah some things to do:

> *Also you shall anoint Jehu the son of Nimshi as king over Israel. And Elisha the son of Shaphat of Abel Meholah you shall anoint as prophet in your place.*

Elijah never anointed Jehu, but he sent one of his prophets to do the job. However, the first thing he did was to seek out Elisha. We all need other people in our lives.

Following these simple and practical steps can make all the difference in our emotional and mental well-being. It worked for Elijah. Try it. You may be pleasantly surprised.

You Will See Greater Things

Jesus saw Nathanael coming toward Him, and said of him, "Behold, an Israelite indeed, in whom is no deceit!"
Nathanael said to Him, "How do You know me?"
Jesus answered and said to him, "Before Philip called you, when you were under the fig tree, I saw you."
Nathanael answered and said to Him, "Rabbi, you are the Son of God! You are the King of Israel!"
Jesus answered and said to him, "Because I said to you, 'I saw you under the fig tree,' do you believe? You will see greater things than these." John 1:47-50

Nathanael was impressed with the fact that Jesus knew him, but Jesus said to him, *"You will see greater things."* There was more:

And He said to him, "Most assuredly, I say to you, hereafter you shall see heaven open, and the angels of God ascending and descending upon the Son of Man."
John 1:51

This sounds strange to us, but the disciples knew exactly what Jesus meant. He was referring to one of the greatest revelations in the Old Testament regarding the Father and His love and character (see Genesis 28). In Jacob's dream, he saw the Father standing at the top of the stairs of Heaven:

> *Then he dreamed, and behold, a ladder was set up on the earth, and its top reached to heaven; and there the angels of God were ascending and descending on it.*
> Genesis 28:12

Jesus was saying that He is the ladder, the open Portal to Heaven and the Source of all angelic activity. Jacob was privileged to see the secret connection with Heaven and the angels ascending and descending the stairs. The Father said:

> *I am the* LORD *God of Abraham your father and the God of Isaac; the land on which you lie I will give to you and your descendants. Also your descendants shall be as the dust of the earth; you shall spread abroad to the west and the east, to the north and the south; and in you and in your seed all the families of the earth shall be blessed. Behold, I am with you.*
> Genesis 28:13-15

God said He would be involved in Jacob's life, and He was. He is always engaged in the lives of His children. His is the unseen hand that will keep us wherever we go.

God would continue to defend Jacob wherever he went, not controlling and not micromanaging, but protecting and defending. Verse 15 concludes:

Behold, I am with you and will keep you wherever you go, and will bring you back to this land; for I will not leave you until I have done what I have spoken to you.

God had a vision for Jacob's future, even his distant future, and promised to be with him regardless. That seemed to be an outrageously bold claim, but He is the Gate, the Way to the Father, the Connection between Heaven and Earth. He is God in the flesh, so He brought Heaven to Earth.

Again, to Nathaniel, Jesus said: *"Most assuredly, I say to you, hereafter you shall see heaven open, and the angels of God ascending and descending upon the Son of Man"* (John 1:51). Jesus is our open Heaven, and He said, "From now on, you shall see Heaven open." Some translations don't even have the word: "henceforth" or "hereafter" like the KJV, but the word *aparti* in this context is translated as "henceforth" and means "from now on." In other words, from now on you will see Heaven open and the angels having access to the events on earth.

The angels, who do the work, will be where Jesus is. Not only will they do the work on the earth; they will finish it and then return to Heaven.

Here Jesus shows that He is the Movable Stairs. These stairs go wherever He goes.

When I was a boy, we used to visit the airport for free entertainment, and I was fascinated with the trucks that had stairs connected to them. Before there were jetways, the driver of those trucks would back up to the plane and place the stairs next to the doors of the fuselage, so when the door opened the passengers could exit the plane. My desire is to bring Jesus, the Ladder, close enough so that people can connect with Him.

He is the Breaker who opens Heaven so that from now on, we have an open Heaven. He opens the way to miracles, He is our Gate or Door to Heaven, and He gives us access to the throne of God.

Why does Jesus mention angels in this passage? Because there is work to do. With God, there is always activity. Our work is the opportunity to connect with the angels and gain their cooperation. Whatever is needed in our day-to-day life becomes a bridge for them to connect to us at the point of our greatest need. Jesus opens the way for angels to do their work.

If you hang around God long enough, you will see His glory (see John 11). He is the Problem Solver. Give your situation to Him. His angels will soon come down like an army of workers to the field. They will be equipped to receive and transmit messages from the Father. This revelation opens our expectations to unbelievable levels.

All the angels are activated through Jesus. Anything that happens in the Kingdom is through Him. Get in Him and stay in Him, and you will see those greater things.

THE CHALLENGE OF ISAIAH 61

When Jesus stood up in the synagogue in His hometown, He declared that Isaiah 61:1-2 was fulfilled in Him. Verse 1 states:

The Spirit of the LORD God is upon Me,
Because the LORD has anointed Me
To preach good tidings to the poor;
He has sent Me to heal the brokenhearted,
To proclaim liberty to the captives,
And the opening of the prison to those who are bound.

Isaiah 61:1

Volumes have been written about Jesus' remarkable anointing to touch individuals' lives, to heal the brokenhearted, to proclaim liberty to the captives, and to preach good tidings to the poor. What humility, for the King of the Universe to start with us rather than first asserting His authority to rule over us.

The Bible shows that He would bring justice. How? By laying down His life. The English judicial system, from which the U.S. system derives, was largely written by Sir William Blackstone (1723-1780) and his colleagues in the eighteenth century. Deeply religious men, they set down the principle that the law should develop over time based upon precedent—literally "trial and error." When an error occurred in a criminal trial, they insisted, it must be noted, and if it was "material," the conviction should be reversed. And what was, to them, the greatest example of a criminal trial which convicted the accused wrongly? It was the trial of Jesus Christ. They considered what they saw as errors in His trial and drew from those errors to write the English law.

What were those errors? Here are just a few examples:

1. The defendant, Jesus, was forced to testify. Therefore, they concluded that no criminal defendant should be coerced to testify.
2. The trial was held in the darkness of night rather than being open to the public. Therefore, they concluded that trials should be public.
3. The trial occurred so quickly that the defendant was not able to mount a proper defense. Therefore, they concluded that every defendant should be given time to respond to the charges against him.
4. The trial was held in front of a single judge rather than a jury of Jesus' peers. Therefore, they concluded that a trial should be conducted before a jury made up of the defendant's peers.

5. The defendant was chained and tortured before being convicted. Therefore, they concluded that no punishment should be meted out until a proper sentence is legally declared.
6. The defendant was never given a clear statement of the charge to enable him to defend Himself. (The Rabbis said, "If He were not guilty, we would not have brought Him to you.") Therefore, they concluded that every defendant had the right to know clearly the charge against him so he could mount a proper defense.
7. The defendant was not given the opportunity to offer any witnesses in his own defense. Therefore, they concluded that every defendant had the right to present witnesses in his favor.

Ironically, by laying down His life, Jesus created a precedent for how a trial should NOT be conducted. His crucifixion was an ugly precedent. Based on this, the justice system in the Western world was forever changed. There is a marked difference in criminal law between countries with a Judeo-Christian heritage from those without such a hstory.

Some say that the tide has turned too far in the opposite direction so defendants are acquitted too easily because of technicalities. The courts have said, however, that it is better for one defendant to be set free on a technicality than for other defendants to be wrongly convicted by a sloppy judicial system.

Isaiah first wrote about the ministry of the Messiah:

> *To proclaim the acceptable year of the* LORD,
> *And the day of vengeance of our God;*
> *To comfort all who mourn,*
> *To console those who mourn in Zion,*
> *To give them beauty for ashes,*
> *The oil of joy for mourning,*
> *The garment of praise for the spirit of heaviness;*
> *That they may be called trees of righteousness,*
> *The planting of the* LORD, *that He may be glorified.*
>
> Isaiah 61:2-3

Isaiah then turned to the impact and transformation to be brought about by Jesus' sacrifice, the impact of the Messiah on society or the fruit of Jesus' labors. God's people are to build something:

> *And they shall rebuild the old ruins,*
> *They shall raise up the former desolations,*
> *And they shall repair the ruined cities,*
> *The desolations of many generations.* Isaiah 61:4

Isaiah showed that God's people would be successful in the world as well as being righteous priests:

Strangers shall stand and feed your flocks,
And the sons of the foreigner
Shall be your plowmen and your vinedressers.
But you shall be named the priests of the LORD,
They shall call you the servants of our God.
You shall eat the riches of the Gentiles,
And in their glory you shall boast.   Isaiah 61:5-6

There will be, Isaiah shows us, a transformation, a reformation, and honor instead of shame:

For I, the LORD, love justice;
I hate robbery for burnt offering;
I will direct their work in truth,
And will make with them an everlasting covenant.
                                                              Isaiah 61:8

There is to be prosperity for our children and grandchildren, the blessing of God crossing over generations:

Their descendants shall be known among the Gentiles,
And their offspring among the people.
All who see them shall acknowledge them,
That they are the posterity whom the LORD has blessed.
                                                              Isaiah 61:9

The results of Jesus's death and resurrection and our entering into His plan brings great joy:

The Challenge of Isaiah 61

I will greatly rejoice in the LORD,
My soul shall be joyful in my God;
For He has clothed me with the garments of salvation,
He has covered me with the robe of righteousness,
As a bridegroom decks himself with ornaments,
And as a bride adorns herself with her jewels.

Isaiah 61:10

The ultimate result is reformation, but this change will occur over time, just as a garden develops over a planting season:

For as the earth brings forth its bud,
As the garden causes the things that are sown in it to spring forth,
So the LORD God will cause righteousness and praise to spring forth before all the nations.   Isaiah 61:11

There is a challenge in this passage. First, for us to be set free with salvation from Jesus (He heals the broken-hearted), but once healed. We can enter into the plans He has for us in His Kingdom. This requires that we grow up, walk with Him, and be changed, being conformed to His image, and impact our world as Christ's ambassadors. What a privilege!

FOOLISHNESS VS WISDOM

Jesus has nothing to do with foolishness. It may be surprising to some to learn that foolishness is mentioned often in the book of Proverbs as a sin. Personally, I have been convicted recently for spending hours watching silly television shows. Similarly, how many of us spend an inordinate amount of time on the internet, moving from one empty video to the next?

Wisdom is in the sight of him who has understanding,
But the eyes of a fool are on the ends of the earth.
Proverbs 17:24

He who follows frivolity is devoid of understanding.
Proverbs 12:11

Proverbs warns us:

O you simple ones, understand prudence,
And you fools, be of an understanding heart.
Listen, for I will speak of excellent things,

FOOLISHNESS VS WISDOM

And from the opening of my lips will come right things;.   Proverbs 8:5-6

Do we speak foolishness? Sadly, I was brought up to do exactly that, but I have learned that it is not God's way:

For my mouth will speak truth;
Wickedness is an abomination to my lips.
All the words of my mouth are with righteousness;
Nothing crooked or perverse is in them.
They are all plain to him who understands,
And right to those who find knowledge. Proverbs 8:7-9

Foolishness is just the opposite of wisdom, which *"is better than rubies":*

Receive my instruction, and not silver,
And knowledge rather than choice gold;
For wisdom is better than rubies,
And all the things one may desire cannot be compared with her.

"I, wisdom, dwell with prudence,
And find out knowledge and discretion."
         Proverbs 8:10-12

MIRACLES IN THE MARKETPLACE

The book of Proverbs not only provides lessons for young men and women on how to grow up and live life; it also teaches us how to govern:

Counsel is mine, and sound wisdom;
I am understanding, I have strength.
By me kings reign,
And rulers decree justice.
By me princes rule, and nobles,
All the judges of the earth.   Proverbs 8:14-16

Solomon shows us that wisdom is attainable if we are willing to forsake foolishness:

I love those who love me,
And those who seek me diligently will find me.
      Proverbs 8:17

Wisdom, Solomon shows us, leads to prosperity and justice:

Riches and honor are with me,
Enduring riches and righteousness.
My fruit is better than gold, yes, than fine gold,
And my revenue than choice silver.
I traverse the way of righteousness,
In the midst of the paths of justice,

FOOLISHNESS VS WISDOM

That I may cause those who love me to inherit wealth,
That I may fill their treasuries.   Proverbs 8: 18-21

If you, like me, had little or no financial inheritance from your parents, this verse should speak to you too. God still promises us an inheritance. Wisdom, in the Person of the Holy Spirit, pre-existed the Earth itself:

The LORD possessed me at the beginning of His way,
Before His works of old.
I have been established from everlasting,
From the beginning, before there was ever an earth.
When there were no depths I was brought forth,
When there were no fountains abounding with water.
Before the mountains were settled,
Before the hills, I was brought forth. Proverbs 8:22-25

The Holy Spirit is also the Author of the Arts:

Then I was beside Him as a master craftsman;
And I was daily His delight,
Rejoicing always before Him,
Rejoicing in His inhabited world,
And my delight was with the sons of men.
                                    Proverbs 8:30-31

Wisdom or foolishness, which will it be?

An Extraordinary Life

Jesus said, *"I have come that they may have life, and they may have it more abundantly"* (John 10:10). This abundant life is so amazing and so vast that it would take a lifetime to learn about all that God has for us. As we have seen, this word *abundant* can also be translated as "extraordinary," so this passage could read: "I have come that they may have an extraordinary life." God has surely allowed me to see Him do some extraordinary things.

Our law firm had the privilege of representing the John Nash Estate. For those who don't know, Nash was the noted professor at Princeton who was the subject of the movie *A Beautiful Mind* starring Russell Crow and Jennifer Connelly. We had the privilege of working with Mr. Nash's son on his father's complex and valuable estate. Among other things, we arranged to sell John Nash's Nobel Prize at auction with Christie's in New York City.

Unfortunately, Mr. Nash died, along with his wife, in a terrible car accident after he had received another prize for his work with "Game Theory." The Nashes had divorced and then remarried, but their two wills had never been coordinated. This did not bode well for an amicable resolution of two competing wills. I give all the glory to God for helping us manage this very complex estate successfully. It is God who is the Giver of all wisdom, and wisdom is certainly needed to successfully handle such difficult cases. In the process of working out these wills, we got to know Mr. Nash's son, who appeared in the movie three times.

One of my law partners also wanted a role in the movie as an extra. Unfortunately, he was removed rather unceremoniously. It went something like this:

Russell Crow began a speech as John Nash in one the large auditoriums in Princeton, and the audience could be seen at the bottom of the picture frame. Ron Howard, the Director, suddenly yelled, "CUT!" He walked down the aisle, pointed to my law partner in the audience, and said, "You, your bald head is shining on the bottom of my picture!" My partner was forcibly removed, and Russell Crow started his speech over.

On another occasion, Emily and I received complimentary tickets to attend a Christmas concert at Carnegie Hall in New York City. We were thrilled. You can imagine our surprise when the conductor, our client, walked out on stage to a standing ovation. We hadn't realized he would be directing. (He was just as dramatic when appearing in our office and always expected applause when he came in.) He had won two Grammys, and as a single man with no children, had the heartbreaking problem of trying to figure out who should receive these statues if he should die. He passed away recently, and it made me think about what value such trophies have, since we can't take them with us when we die. All the more reason to build up the treasures kept for us in Heaven which will not pass away (see Matthew 6:19-20).

This extraordinary life begins now and lasts for an eternity.

SINGLE OR MARRIED?

One day many years ago, after I had given a message at church, one of my Christian brothers came up to me and said, "You're not qualified to teach because you're single. You will never experience true suffering until you're married!" and he was dead serious. Well, I hadn't experienced *his* kind of suffering, but single people know a different type of suffering—the loneliness, the emptiness, and the injurious comments both spoken and unspoken like: 'What's wrong with him [or her]?"

In my case, I simply had not yet found someone who loved Jesus as much as I did, and I think that's the experience of many Christian singles. If they have integrity, they want the real thing. However, God is a good Matchmaker. I highly recommend a book by Derek and Ruth Prince entitled *God Is a Matchmaker*.[1]

One day, while I was visiting my sister in California, I received a call from some close friends, Bill and Carol Grady. They said "While you're out here, you should look up Emily. She's a blonde, and she's normal!" I was intrigued.

---
1. Ada, Michigan (Chosen Books: 2011)

Unfortunately, since I had to return to New Jersey that day, I would have to call Emily from home. After working up the courage for a month, I called Emily during a workday. At first, she thought it was a call for her boss, who was also an attorney, but she soon realized the call was for her. We struck up a frequent phone relationship (no internet back then) and talked for hours at a time. Frankly, I didn't think the relationship would come to anything because of the distance, and so the calls gradually became more infrequent.

Then one day I sensed there was something amiss in my relationship with the Lord. Have you ever had that feeling? I got in my conference room at the office and sat alone for a while. "Lord, what's wrong?" I asked.

He said just one word to me: "California." This, of course, could have meant many things. Was God saying that I should expand my practice to California? Somehow I knew instinctively that He meant I should visit Emily. I called her and made arrangements to fly out there to visit her in Irvine.

On my way to Emily's office, I bought some flowers, but, still unsure of what might happen, I left them in the car. Thankfully, when I walked in to meet Emily, she greeted me with a big hug. It was love at first sight for me, and during my days there in California, we visited Newport Beach, Rodeo Drive, Venice Beach, San Diego and Santa Monica.

SINGLE OR MARRIED?

When I returned home, I sent Emily a "tennis bracelet" and a round-trip ticket to visit me over Christmas. Fortunately, she accepted. We spent time in New York City, at places like Windows on the World (a restaurant that occupied the 106th and 107th floors of one of the Twin Towers) and Times Square and did some window shopping on Madison Avenue.

I took Emily to my office in Princeton and there I confided in her my plans for our future. I took her to see the sights in Philadelphia, and we went together to the church I attended at the time.

I visited California again in January to propose and, after several more cross-country visits, Emily and I were married at the Vineyard Church in Anaheim in May of 1998. We have been happily married for twenty-six years. She has been not only a precious wife to me, but also an important partner in the business.

An Amazing Birthday Present

By 2001, managing the Princeton office as a sole practitioner had become very difficult. I was handling more than a hundred real estate transactions per year, about the same number of estate plans and several probate matters. It was a nightmare trying to train and keep enough staff to handle our very busy practice. Emily was now working in the firm with me, and she was the reason for its success, but the press of work was exceedingly difficult and stressful for both of us.

One afternoon, as I was working at my desk just before my birthday, I opened a gift from Emily, and the Lord said, "I have a birthday present for you too." I didn't know what He meant by this and no present appeared immediately, but I decided to watch for it and see what would transpire.

Not long after that, I learned that another law firm was looking at my rented office space with the intention of taking it over. This began a month-long conversation with them about sharing offices and merging. The connection with this firm solved some of the staffing problems and administrative issues I was having, it greatly decreased the stress, and was definitely a glorious birthday present from the Lord.

Truth be told, the partners of the large firm believed they would simply absorb me and take over my practice, but just the opposite happened. My side of the practice flourished and theirs decreased. I helped pay off their debt, and God continued to bless my side of the practice. Eventually, they all moved on, and I took it over. I give all the glory to God who teaches us how to prosper. He gives us thoughts on how to succeed. He gives us physical strength when we have no more strength of our own.

God doesn't dole out prosperity like a gum ball machine, and it's not magic. Yes, money can appear in our bank account supernaturally, but that has not been my experience. My experience has been more along the lines of getting ideas for how to grow the business, receiving energy and passion to work hard, and receiving ideas about how to explain complex tax issues to clients so they can know what they need to do.

God's Spirit also gives me knowledge of complex trusts to help clients with special needs children. He shows me how to make the probate process easier, less expense, and with lower taxes, and He gives me ideas on how to resolve family conflicts before they get to court. These solutions definitely do not come because I have some great ability or wisdom. Quite the contrary! They come because I am connected with our God, who is all ALL WISDOM.

As I noted at the outset, because the Holy Spirit gives me an unfair advantage, some have called me The Miracle Man for the results I've obtained, but I have to insist: Only God does miracles! All the glory belongs to Him!

Part 2

Visions and Prophecies from the Holy Spirit

Introduction

Through the years, aside from my work as an attorney, the Lord has given me the privilege to see visions and give prophecies at various Christian gatherings. Early on, I got in the habit of writing these prophecies down and have chosen some that I thought might be a blessing and included them in this book.

Although prophecies are for a specific people at a specific time, they can also have a positive impact on all of us, *"for there is no partiality with God"* (Romans 2:11). These prophecies have had a profound effect on my own life and my understanding of the Scriptures, and I trust they will be a blessing to you too.

Alexander Watson

A Ribbon from Heaven

On Sunday morning, April 15, 2015, during a worship service, I looked up and saw something very strange in the Spirit. I saw symbols, numbers, and letters coming down in a jumble, falling down from Heaven. At first, I didn't understand what this all meant, but after a while I was able to understand that it was computer language. This jumble of letters and numbers began to form themselves into a steady, strong, unbroken ribbon of computer language.

Then I looked down and saw us sitting at our computers typing up messages on the internet. Our efforts were feeble, primitive attempts at communications on websites, and in emails, and blogs. Our messages were pitiful, weak, and intermittent. To me, it actually looked like we were sending up smoke signals much as the American Indians had done in another time to convey messages from village to village. To the Lord, I saw, our work on the internet was very primitive indeed.

But then I saw our messages join with the ribbon of computer language from Heaven, and they turned to a gold stream of communication. I believe the gold represented God's glory and permanency.

Next, I saw the ribbon divide and go in four different directions and travel all over the earth. A confirming scripture can be found in Psalm 19:1-6:

> *The heavens declare the glory of God;*
> *And the firmament shows His handiwork.*
> *Day unto day utters speech,*
> *And night unto night reveals knowledge.*
> *There is no speech nor language*
> *Where their voice is not heard.*
> *Their line has gone out through all the earth,*
> *And their words to the end of the world.*
> *In them He has set a tabernacle for the sun,*
> *Which is like a bridegroom coming out of his chamber,*
> *And rejoices like a strong man to run its race.*
> *Its rising is from one end of heaven,*
> *And its circuit to the other end;*
> *And there is nothing hidden from its heat.*

I believe God is going to use our primitive internet to bring His Word to the whole Earth.

Different Mountaintops

Emily and I joined a volunteer team to minister in the healing rooms. On one particular occasion, there were seven of us on the team. During worship, as we were preparing ourselves for the challenges of the day, the Lord took us to Heaven. We were on the mountaintops looking down at the clouds. Here we had a unique view of the Kingdom below. We could see that it was a place of trees, fields, and streams and of water in abundance.

Then I saw something unusual. I saw that the Lord had placed each one of us on a different mountaintop. Each person was standing on his or her mountaintop, and as each of us looked down, we saw different aspects of the Kingdom because we all had different perspectives. One member of the team was a researcher in the pharmaceutical industry, one worked at Princeton University, one was a paralegal, one worked at a book store, one was a lawyer, and one was a homemaker. We were all from different fields of service.

The popular book by Johnny Enlow, *The Seven Mountain Prophecy*,[1] had recently impacted the Church. In the book,

1. Littlestown, PA (Creation House: 2008)

Johnny had highlighted what he called the seven mountains of society or spheres of influence in our culture: Government, Education, Media, Family, Economy, Arts & Entertainment, and Religion. His challenge was that we should be preparing our Christian young people for service in all these areas of influence. "God is calling His people," he wrote, "to go out and take ground in each of these mountains." And here we were, seven very different people, from very different walks of life, on seven different mountains, looking down with seven different perspectives. In that moment, I was reminded of Proverbs 9:1:

> *Wisdom has built her house,*
> *She has hewn out her seven pillars.*

Clearly God was in control of our work that day.

AN OFFERING CONVERTED TO A BLESSING

In November of 2007, during a church service, I watched as someone prayed over the offering. As I watched, I saw in the Spirit the money in the basket catch fire. The fire increased, and I saw it transformed to a large caldron of oil—beautiful, rich red oil which burned. I saw the tithes and offerings as fuel that had turned into a large caldron of burning oil.

Then I saw two angels lift the caldron of oil and carry it up a narrow flight of stairs up a tower directly above us. The stairs wound their way up the tower. The two angels opened a window in Heaven, looked out on us, and smiled. They were full of joy. Then I saw them pour the oil down on us.

As the oil came down, it immediately changed in character. It came down in many different forms, some in paper, some in gold flakes, and some in leaves. This represented the many forms of heavenly blessings, depending on what each of us needed. For some, it was healing; for some, it was a financial blessing; for some, it was a breakthrough; and for others, it was a relationship blessing. The angels were so joyful in sending down exactly what we needed. This reminded me of the words of Malachi:

> "Bring all the tithes into the storehouse,
> That there may be food in My house,
> And try Me now in this,"
> Says the LORD of hosts,
> "If I will not open for you the windows of heaven
> And pour out for you such blessing
> That there will not be room enough to receive it."
>
> Malachi 3:10

The Bible doesn't say what kind of blessing. The favor of our loving heavenly Father comes down to us in many types of blessings, depending on what we need at the moment.

The Tablets of Your Heart
Given at His Hands Fellowship

The question was asked — WHY GO THROUGH THIS PROCESS?

I saw the Lord standing in front of you, and He was able to read the tablets of your heart almost like a computer screen. Then I saw you voluntarily reach into your own heart and pull out a book from the hidden places. This book is the recording of all the hurts and all the difficult things you've been through. It was your whole history. I saw Him take the book and sit down on the curb and read it.

He read with great interest and great compassion. When He read some pages, He said, "I can really use this!" Other pages He tore out and dropped into the sea of forgetfulness. After reading it all with great compassion, He stood up and smiled at you and handed the book back to you.

Then, again with great compassion, He explained things to you about your history. He gave you practical wisdom on how to deal with the things of your past and how to deal with your present circumstances. I then saw you tuck the book back into your heart, and He said, "You can bring out those stories whenever you want to."

So, why do you have to go though this process? The Lord would say: "As you allow Me to 'read' you, you will be able to read others accurately and with compassion. You will know which stories (of theirs) to use (for their benefit) and which stories to drop into the sea of forgetfulness. You will be able to listen to others and give practical solutions with compassion.

Jeremiah, Ezekiel, Daniel and Jesus

In a Chuck Pierce meeting in October of 2004, while we were worshipping, I saw the stream of the Holy Spirit come into the meeting from the front. His presence kept rising in the meeting, until He had filled the room. This reminded me of Ezekiel 47 where the river rose so high that you could no longer swim in it. It covered us completely. Then, at that moment, we were all caught up into Heaven.

In Heaven, a man met us. I asked the Lord who this man was. The Lord did not say a word, but the man himself answered and introduced himself as "Jeremiah." He was no longer "the Weeping Prophet," because he had met the Messiah, the King. He was excited and spoke to us about the promise God had given him that he wrote down in Jeremiah 33:3. He wanted us to know that this promise was for us as well:

Call to Me, and I will answer you, and show you great and mighty things, which you do not know.

To always remind us of this promise, Jeremiah wrote "33:3" on the palms of our hands. He then introduced us to another man. This man was Ezekiel.

Ezekiel sat down beside the river, and we sat on the riverbank behind and above him, looking over his shoulders. He gestured with his hand toward our left, pointing to the Temple in the distance. We saw the water flowing toward us from the throne, and the river became deeper and deeper as it approached. He said, "Make sure God's people know that the scripture in the forty-seventh chapter of my book is for this time and not for another. The river represents the flow of the Holy Spirit for continuous provision and healing. It is His nature, and the scripture is for THIS time." (So we have revelation from Jeremiah 33:3 and provision from Ezekiel 47.)

Ezekiel then introduced us to the next man. This was Daniel. Daniel sat down on a chair, and we stood behind him looking over his shoulder at the book in his lap. He showed us the portion of his book in which he spoke about the Church in the end times. He said, "Make sure God's people know this is for now — the Church in warfare, marching forth in power. It is for this time and not another."

Now all three men bowed down in worship, and I looked around to discover why. I saw that the valley below us was filled with people worshipping joyfully. Then I saw the Lamb of God approaching, and we all bowed down in worship together. The Lord Himself spoke and said, "This is My time, and it is YOUR time too. It is the time for the Church."

SNOW IN THE SPRING
GIVEN AT PRINCETON FELLOWSHIP CHURCH
MARCH OF 1989 OR 1990

When it snows in the spring, you have confidence that because the earth is warmer and the sun is up for longer periods of time, even if the snow is several inches deep, it will only stay on the ground for a few hours. It will melt quickly. In fact, you don't cancel events, and you are certain you will be able to return home without a problem. The quickly melting snow will soon disappear.

It is the same with that evil thing that seems to be clutching you and won't let go. You can have confidence that as you keep walking with Jesus, it won't be able to hang on for long. It will drop off. It must let go. It will not stay. It will go away as surely as the snowfall in springtime.

Resist the devil and he will flee from you.   James 4:7

The Bottom of the Cross
Given 11/20/2016 at Ewing Worship Church

During worship, I saw the bottom of the cross. I saw the blood soaking into the rough wood. I saw it run down the wood and onto the ground. I saw it touch and then soak the ground and disappear into the mud. All seemed to be lost.

When Jesus died, it seemed as if all had been lost. It seemed as if the blood that was spilled there had disappeared into the ground forever, and that was the end of it. Of course, that was not true.

Just as it seemed as if that blood Jesus shed was lost and forgotten, some of you feel as if your suffering has gone unnoticed, that no one knows the suffering you have gone through. It even seems as if God has forgotten. But NONE of the tears you have shed have been lost. None of your pain has been forgotten by God. He has collected every tear. He was with you in the mud and the blood, and nothing has escaped His attention.

When Cain killed Abel, he thought he had gotten rid of him (and some people thought they got rid of you), but God said that He could hear Abel's blood crying out from the ground (see Hebrews 11:14). Just as God heard Abel's blood speaking, the blood of Jesus still speaks today. The Bible says that the blood of Jesus speaks a better word than the blood of Abel (see Hebrews 12:24). The voice of that blood will never be shut up, lost, or forgotten.

Then I saw Jesus, and He was alive again. I saw the holes in His hands. I saw Him provide you with new clothing—elegant and regal. I saw Him giving you a new life and a new hope. Receive it today!

Distributing Mantles
During Healing Team Worship 4/28/2012

I saw the Father distributing mantles, like robes. I saw Him providing clothing to each of us, like a loving Father providing for His children.

Elisha worked hard, desperately following Elijah, hoping against hope that Elijah's mantle would fall on him when his master was taken up. But what he only hoped for has been bought for us with the precious blood of Jesus.

When Jesus ascended back to the Father, He promised that the Holy Spirit would come as a mantle, a covering of power. He told His disciples that they should wait in Jerusalem until they were clothed with this power (see Acts 1:4).

When the Holy Spirit came on the Day of Pentecost, Peter said *"For the promise is to you and your children and for all who are afar off"* (Acts 2:39). This anointing of power is not only for us, but also for our children, for all who desire it. The Father has a mantle for all.

We no longer need an Elijah, because Jesus has come and given us His Spirit. Through Jesus' death and resurrection, He paid for it all. The Father now provides a mantle or robe of anointing for each of us, and it fits and is comfortable. Then, as we grow, He provides an ever larger and expanding mantle for us.

A Man Healed

In 1971, during my freshman year at Princeton, I awoke one morning from a vivid dream and shot out of bed. As I stood there, I found myself standing on a slight hill looking down an embankment and seeing Jesus from behind. I only saw His back, but I could see that He was healing a man who had been using a walker. I saw Jesus pulling the walker away, and the man was healed. Then I saw Jesus continue to walk to the right to the next person. He never looked up at me, but I saw Him walking on.

The weekend following I visited what was called "The Barn Church" at Simsbury, Connecticut. I had taken the train from Princeton for the weekend, possibly Thanksgiving. The pastor reported at the Barn that a man had been healed that very same Thursday evening of not being able to walk without a walker.

THE MARRIAGE CEREMONY
GIVEN AT A REGIONAL PRAYER MEETING IN NEW JERSEY 5/8/2011

I saw the Bride of Christ, the Church, kept in a secret place, and she was preparing herself, as it says in the book of Revelation (see Revelation 19:7). Then I saw her turn, and like a bride on her wedding day, slowly take half steps down the aisle toward the front of the church, her dress flowing and flawless.

Then the Lord said, "There has been a time when the church has been sequestered, hidden, preparing for that great day, but the time is coming very soon, and now is, when she will begin to walk down the aisle. Every eye will be on her—some in disbelief, some in criticism, but mostly in awe—just the same way a congregation turns to look at a bride walking down the aisle on her wedding day. Everyone will be in awe of her beauty and her authority and power." (I saw flashes of lightning coming from her hands.)

As she continued to slowly walk down the aisle, I saw the nations in her belly. When the Bride reached the front of the church, the King of Kings stood there to lovingly receive her.

THE MARRIAGE CEREMONY

As in any wedding, gifts were given. The Groom placed a crown on her head, and the bride, with a sweeping motion, drew her arm from left to right across her body and raised her right hand over her head. Out of her belly came the nations of the Earth.

I saw her hold all the nations of the earth in her right hand, held high over her head. It looked like a globe, but I could see all the continents at once. Each nation was alive and moving and changing as she presented the nations to Jesus Christ as her gift:

> *The kingdoms of this world have become the kingdoms of our Lord and of His Christ, and He shall reign forever and ever!* Revelation 11:5

> *Ask of Me, and I will give You*
> *The nations for Your inheritance,*
> *And the ends of the earth for Your possession.*
> Psalm 2:8

> *Arise, O God, judge the earth;*
> *For You shall inherit all nations.* Psalm 82:8

That day is rapidly approaching.

TRUST THE LIGHTHOUSE
GIVEN 5/2/2004

"The boat is large and stable, the sails are full, and this sailboat is moving. I will bring you to the desired destination, but I want to bring you to the destination I want for you.

"You can see the next lighthouse ahead. Some want to hug the shore, but I want you to go out into the open waters. The open water is safer because it is deeper, and the bottom of the boat won't run against the rocks. To you, the shoreline seems safer because it's closer to the land, but I tell you there are hidden rocks there.

"There are those who want to be near the shore, following religious rules, the traditions of men and legalisms. These all give a sense of security, but I tell you, 'Go out into the deep where I am and where the Holy Spirit is. It is safer.'

"There are times out on the open ocean when you don't see land or the lighthouse, but you are to follow your last guidance and direction. Keep on that prescribed course. As you keep traveling, you will see one lighthouse and then the next. The lighthouse is secure and made of stones. Trust it to lead you to safety."

The Receiver
Given 1/5/2012

As we worshiped, I saw us standing on a small hill overlooking a valley. We could see trees all around, green grass, and streams. This represented the Kingdom of God. There was a mist that came in waves and watered the land and then stopped for a while.

In the distance, I saw a man. He was hunched over and clearly hopeless. He was so empty you could see right through him. I recognized that he was a "receiver."[1]

The man began walking toward us and looked to our left, his right. As we turned to the left, we could see heavenly beings standing beside us. Some were average height, but some were as much as nine feet tall. Each one was different in appearance and in clothing. These celestial beings were clad in royal raiment, very bright gold robes. Some had tall crown-like headpieces. The gold was very bright, and they themselves were so bright that gold light emanated from them. The gold actually radiated light onto the ground below our feet.

---

1. *Receiver* was a term used by this group for a person who desired more of God and, therefore, wanted prayer.

The man began to walk up the hill toward us. Curiously, we noticed that he was not looking at us, but to our left. He was drawn by something or someone that he couldn't seem to see. He couldn't see the heavenly creatures, but he was drawn by their glory.

His face was lit up with the reflected glory of these beings, and his countenance began to change. A smile came across his face as his hopelessness turned to joy.

In his hand he had a tablet, and he was studiously taking copious notes. This "receiver" was acquiring skills for life. He garnered two things from this encounter. First, a bit of the glory, and second, knowledge and practical skills to take with him.

The man then turned to go on his way, and he began to actually skip for joy. We stood on the hill unmoved, and the celestial beings remained next to us. One of them turned to you with a gold tablet in his hands—bright, bright gold that radiated light—and he spoke with the voice of a lion. As I looked down on the tablet, it looked like a book with an ornate gold cover front and back unlike any other I had ever seen. Its bright gold radiated light.

He gave the tablet to you, just as the angels gave a scroll to Ezekiel and to the apostle John. You held it to your chest, and it became part of you.

I asked the Lord what this signified. He said, "It is the gift of solutions to problems you haven't even encountered yet. It is a gift of greater revelation. It is a new anointing. It is revelation of the future and understanding of the past. It is the gift of answers to questions that have not yet even arisen. The past is yours, the present is yours, and the future is yours" (see 1 Corinthians 3:21-22).

FACES LIKE LIONS
GIVEN AT EWING WORSHIP CHURCH 10/15/2016

During worship, I saw the Lord. With one sweep of His arm, He swept away all the sin, all the things of the past, all the words spoken against you, and all the rejection you had suffered. He did this for your sake.

And He says to you this day: "It is the Father's good pleasure to give you the Kingdom in many different manifestations. He has given gifts—diamonds and rubies. To some of you, He has given crowns.

I saw Him setting the table for you with many good things. I saw some of you with faces like lions, some as intercessors, and some speaking the Word of God to the needy world and doing it fearlessly, like lions.

STANDING AT THE RED SEA
GIVEN 11/17/2016 AT EWING WORSHIP CHURCH

Some of you are standing at the Red Sea. You say, "But I got saved a year ago, or five years ago, or fifty years ago, so how could this happen? How could this happen?" It is truly an impossible situation you are facing, impossible, and yet the Lord says to you, "Step forward and cross!"

As I step forward, the wind whips up, and I can see a giant wall of water form on the left and the right. The wall stands about thirty feet high on each side. As I look up to the top of the wall, I can see the wind is whipping up the water at the top, but the wall stays in place.

I look down and notice that I am walking in mud, which sticks to my shoes. The walls are tall and intimidating, but the Lord says: "Keep moving FORWARD! The victory, the Kingdom, is on the other side. Don't look to the right or to the left. Just keep walking. The Kingdom is ahead. The victory is ahead. I am the only One who brings victory," says the Lord!

A Trail To the Villages
Given at His Hands Church

During worship, I saw the Lord walking away, leading along a trail. I said in my flesh, "Why are You going? The Body of Christ is here! Over there, Mr. Smith is the 'heart,' over there, Mrs. White is the 'hand,' and over there, Miss Jones is the 'nose.' The Body of Christ is right here, and not in the outside world. Why are You leaving?" He didn't say a word but just kept walking away.

I started to follow Him on a narrow trail through the jungle. He still didn't look back. Then He started to run, and I ran after Him. He came to a clearing where there was a village. He ran from house to house. At each house He touched it briefly, and a flame ignited on the roof. It was the flame of the Holy Spirit.

We went from house to house, and as we touched each house, a flame arose from the top. He said "This is what you have been called to do, to bring the flame of the Holy Spirit to the villages. And there are many other villages yet to touch."

WAVES

I saw an extremely large wave coming in toward us. It is not a coincidence that Hawaii and California have seen record-breaking waves in the past few weeks (the tsunami of March 11, 2011). This is a sign of the mighty move of the Holy Spirit which is coming. The Holy Spirit will come in with unprecedented power and miracles. We will see Him do things that we have never seen before.

I saw a man caught up in the curl. He was spread-eagled, upside down, and dwarfed by the size of the wave. The wave may also turn some of you upside down, but remember: this is still the gentle Holy Spirit who loves you.

With any large wave, there is a powerful undertow, and some of you are looking down at your feet. You can feel the sand slipping away. It's as if the place where you stand is disappearing from beneath you. This creates some uncertainty, but don't be afraid. This is just a sign of the coming wave. Some will try to run away from the wave, but they will not be able to do so. It will touch everyone.

Do not define the work of the Holy Spirit by your own understanding, but let the work of the Holy Spirit inform your understanding. He will do greater miracles that all may marvel (see John 5:20).

Claim this word as your own today.

ARMY OF GOD
GIVEN 11/19/06

I saw the Lord stopping to care for a man who had been injured and left by the side of the road. The Lord was like the Good Samaritan and sat beside the man to care for him. I saw Him lay hands on the man with infinite care and love. I saw the man's heart respond to this love, and he was healed. I don't know whether it was a physical or emotional healing, but I saw the man's physical heart turn red and respond to the Lord's touch.

The Lord seemed to have an infinite amount of time to spend with the man. He got him up on his feet and took him to an army tent marked with a red cross, and there God's people were to continue the healing process. I saw the Lord bring in many other injured people who needed physical and emotional healing.

I saw the man who had been healed walk out the back of the Red Cross tent and walk up the hill to join an encampment. He walked as if he had been raised from the dead. He was completely healed. He, who had been without hope, was now alive unto God. I saw him walk boldly up that hill and join the army.

Miracles in the Marketplace

The army? Let me explain. I saw a vast encampment, as far as the eye could see, on the side of a gently sloping hill. It was actually a group of church camps made up of people from many different denominations. They were dressed in ordinary clothes and were fellowshipping together in the cool of the evening. The tents were desert style, with canopies overhead, but without side curtains. There was fellowship and interaction between churches.

Each church had a flag representing their denomination, but while each flag differed, they all had some red or crimson on it. This represented the fact that each group acknowledged the blood of Jesus Christ shed on Calvary. The other colors on the denominational flags had faded to white. The differences had faded into insignificance.

In the great, great distance to the right of this vast encampment, I saw a lone Rider approaching on a white horse. Instinctively, I knew it was the Lord. As the horse and Rider passed by each encampment, the people all worshipped Him.

When the wind shifted, I heard worship music coming from one camp and then another. Then I heard something which stood out. It was worship in Hebrew from another source. This surprised me.

Behind the encampment to the left, directly behind the encampments, I saw the source of the Hebrew worship. It was a permanent structure, like a fortress or very large bunker with no windows. The people inside were not aware of the other encampment, nor of the lone Rider. They flew the Israeli flag. This represented the nation of Israel and the Jewish people. Most had not yet recognized the King of Kings, the Messiah, and yet I heard worship music from the fortress, worship unto God.

Then I saw the horse and Rider approaching. The horse was restive, and the Rider was awesome. With a staff in His right hand, He quietly rode by the troops.

I shut down the vision, as I often do, so I don't share anything that is just from my own imagination (see Ezekiel 13:2-3 and Jeremiah 23:16 and 26), and I set it aside to see if it would just go away, but it came back. Days later, while I was stuck in traffic, the vision of the horse and Rider appeared again. The horse was now rearing up right in front of me, and this startled me. The Messiah, Jesus Christ, sat on the horse right above me.

I looked at His face, and it had an intensity. His eyes were flaming as if they were on fire (see Revelation 19:12). He was looking over the church group, not with condemnation or judgment, just with intensity, like a general steeling his troops for battle, and with an expectation that His people would do their duty to Him.

His eyes caught mine, and it rocked me to the bone. There was a seriousness, an intensity, and a purpose in His gaze. Then He said to all of us, "If you are willing, stand with Me. I am coming back soon, and My reward is with Me. Just stand with Me."

As He looked out over that vast army, He fixed His gaze on one camp and then another. When He did this, the style of worship shifted from quiet songs to loud roars. Each section He looked at would begin to shake, and a great sound arose from that particular group.

He stood and shook the earth;
He looked and startled the nations.   Habakkuk 3:6

Then everything began to rattle, and a deafening sound of worship came forth. It was not just from the musicians and not just from the people of God. Even the rocks begin to shake.

But He answered and said to them, "If these should keep silent, the stones would immediately cry out.
                                                                                    Luke 19:40

In that moment, I realized this was the type of power that could have shaken the walls of Jericho so much that they collapsed. They could not stand.

Then I saw the fortress of Israel open up from the top. The people inside still did not see the Messiah, but they heard the sound and said to each other, "What is this sound that shakes the earth? We have not heard worship like this before." It was, to them, easily identifiable as being the same as their worship.

Then the Lord said: "This is the sound that will awaken My people, Israel, the sound of worship. My people are asleep, but I will wake them up as one man. The alarm will sound when the time is right, and they will come to Me," says the Lord. "I will do it when the time is right."

SCROLLS IN HEAVEN
GIVEN AT THE MCCARTNEY HOME GROUP 5/19/2011

During worship, the Lord took me to a corner of Heaven, and I saw many things that I did not understand. What I saw was this: The floor, the color of milky quartz, was hard and sloped. In the great distance I could see the earth below.

Then, to my right, I saw a woman dressed in an ordinary white dress. Somehow I knew she was an intercessor. She stood, making declarations and motioned to the earth.

> *But God, who is rich in mercy, because of His great love with which He loved us, even when we were dead in trespasses, make us alive together with Christ(by grace you have been saved), and raised us up together and MADE US SIT TOGETHER IN HEAVENLY PLACES WITH CHRIST JESUS.*
>
> Ephesians 2:4-6, Emphasis Mine

To her right (my left) there appeared several scrolls in mid air, but nothing was written on them. They were blank, as if waiting for words to be written on them.

Then I could see that she was declaring something and motioning with her hand, but I could not hear her. Every time she made a declaration, words appeared on the scrolls from right to left. What she spoke immediately appeared on the scrolls, and these declarations generated the acts of the people of God.

Then I saw each scroll one by one shoot down to different places on the earth, and as they went, they multiplied. This represents praying and declaring a thing so that Heaven comes to Earth.

Our Father in heaven,
Hallowed be Your name.
Your Kingdom come.
Your will be done
On earth as it is in heaven.   Matthew 6:9-10

"It is for you to walk in signs, wonders, and miracles that have been set out for you to do. So walk in them. I am with you," says the Lord, "and will accomplish through you the things that I have spoken to you."

THE SKULL

I, along with a friend, was taken in a vision to stand in a shallow cave or ledge. We were young children in the vision and didn't know where we were. We saw a drop of blood fall from the edge of the rock over our heads, and it splattered as it hit the pock-marked stone ceiling above us. Another drop of blood dripped down and then another.[1]

As we watched, we saw a massive, overwhelming flow of blood which hit the rock ceiling and flowed down in front of us. It was then we realized we were standing on Calvary's hill just below the cross. We stretched to look up, but we could only see the foot of the cross. The scene was so holy and so horrible that we sat and wept like children because we knew our Friend, Jesus, was on that cross and we could not stop what was taking place. We didn't understand, but we knew He did it willingly and because He was our Friend. We also knew that He was going through this because of our sins.

---

1. I've seen photos of Golgatha (translated as "skull"), the rock outcropping in the shape of a skull where Jesus was crucified. Under this massive rock formation, there are many shallow caves or ledges on the side of the hill, sheltered from the massive rock above.

We sat crying for a long time, not daring to look up, but after a while the sun came out, and I peered over the ledge. I was expecting to see a cross, but it was gone. In its place, I saw a tall, stainless-steel I-beam which seemed to go up to Heaven. I walked around it, asking the Lord what it was. Finally, I was given to understand that it was a stake – a tent peg, or in Hebrew, a *vav* (see Isaiah 22:23).

Then the Lord said, "I have removed the sin of this land in a single day (see Zechariah 3:9). With this one act I have secured (pegged) your future. I have nailed the past to the cross. I have secured your healing and your provision. I have staked My claim to redeem men. I have paid the price.

"Do not fear the future, for I will be with you. Do not dwell in the past, for I am no longer there. Just as Jael struck the head of the enemy king, Sisera, with a tent peg (see Judges 4:21 and 5:26), I have destroyed the enemy."

Part 3

An Invitation

MY INVITATION

You may not know the Lord, or you may have just met Him. In either case, I want to introduce you to Him and challenge you to go further with Him. I asked Him into my heart and life when I was just thirteen, and I knew Him as a new Friend and Savior immediately. It was experiential and profound. He said,

> *Behold I stand at the door and knock. If anyone hears my voice and opens the door I will come in and eat with Him and he with me.*   Revelation 3:21

That was fifty-eight years ago, and I remember it as if it were yesterday. I suddenly wanted to tell everyone about my newfound Friend. He changed my life, and He is more real to me today than ever, and my love for Him is greater today than ever.

If you have not asked Him into your life, you can do so now, and the pages of this book will come alive to you since He is, in fact, real.

When I first asked Jesus into my heart, I was not sure that He *was* real. Either He really was the living Son of God, or this whole "Christian thing" was a big hoax. Fortunately, He can be tested and proven. I have called on Him in life's crises, and He has always answered.

If you have already made a commitment to Christ, these pages will challenge you to go further — into the deep, into the challenging waters of relationship with none other than the King of Kings. This book is about my journey, but Jesus challenges each and every one of us. He prods us to go further and even to die to our own selves to find His life instead. I have tested Him and found Him true to His Word every time. Why not give Him a chance in your life as well?

AUTHOR CONTACT

You may contact Alexander Watson directly at:

AWatson085@gmail.com

Alexander Watson, Esq.
Dumont & Watson, PC
600 Alexander Road, Suite 1-1
Princeton, NJ 08540

www.ingramcontent.com/pod-product-compliance
Lightning Source LLC
Chambersburg PA
CBHW041925090426
42743CB00020B/3437